EVERY WHIT WHOLE

MICHAEL DRURY

EVERY WHIT WHOLE

the adventure of spiritual healing

DODD, MEAD & COMPANY NEW YORK

Printed in the United States of America

1 2 3 4 5 6 7 8 9 10

Library of Congress Cataloging in Publication Data

Drury, Michael.

Every whit whole.

1. Faith-cure. I. Title.

BT732.5.D78 615'.852 78-18389

ISBN 0-396-07578-9

preface

To write of Jesus Christ when one has no credentials except delight, faith, and a decent education is a highly risky enterprise. Somebody somewhere is going to get mad. Quite likely, a whole lot of somebodies. Such anger is a kind of cheering thing. Nobody gets mad over something that does not matter to him, and that people care about Jesus is a refreshing fact in today's world.

I am a writer by trade and an inquirer into things spiritual by inclination, and this book has for many years circled around my typewriter trying to get itself written. I have long felt that to each person to whom Christ Jesus is Lord and Teacher, there is a fifth gospel, the one that person lives into reality through the impact of the other four upon him. If that is true, then each of us has a right, almost an obligation, to his own delineation of the biblical record.

My interest in Christianity is by no means confined to Jesus' healings, but they are an aspect of his ministry that has seemed to me somewhat neglected. I mean healings of physical disorders that would today be turned over to the medical profession. So far as I know, all Christian churches accept physical healing by spiritual means, but the only one I am aware of that does so to the exclusion of medical assistance is Christian Science. Some, at least, of the healings recorded by that denomination have been verified by reputable physicians. This is also true of spiritual healings experienced by other Christians. Not all of these people can be merely deluded.

Bodily healing is part of the Gospel as we have it, and I wanted to explore its causes and meaning for myself. I found it high adventure. I have tried to stay away from doctrinal viewpoints, although as a friend said when I first proposed this book, there is no such thing as a nondenominational examination of anything concerning Jesus. That made me laugh, but I knew he was right.

Some of my ideas may raise the eyebrows of scholars and theologians. I ask their indulgence. It was not my intention to make wild and arbitrary interpretations of Scripture, nor to disparage any doctrine. Rather, I wished to sit down with one other person at a time, curious as am I about these matters, and toss ideas around. I hold with both my hands and all my heart to the promise that where two or three are gathered together in his name, there he comes.

contents

1 why heal in the first place?

It takes a long time to make an idea really one's own. The French existentialist Albert Camus said it took ten to twelve years, but I think that's only to find out what it is you are after. Ideas lodge in one's mind and go on shaping themselves over a lifetime. There are not many ideas available to any one person, three or four at most. An idea can assume countless forms, but upon examination one discovers that it is the same idea repeated in a hundred different configurations.

An idea that has flickered like heat lightning around the edges of my mind for several decades has to do with the healings brought about in Bible times, especially the healings of Christ Jesus. There was nothing noble in my interest—I had no great desire to serve others—but neither was it self-seeking. I was not ill, nor was anyone in my family. For some reason, or no reason, I was curious.

As a child, I had two or three experiences that seemed to me then, and still do, both mysterious and wonderful. They were not healings, though I know now they were of the same nature. I should term them encounters with the infinite. I believe all children undergo somewhat mystical experiences, then lose them in the press of daily living or are taught to disregard them. I lived close to the sea and deep forests and animals, and I was already in my secret heart a storyteller, so for me these curious events remained vivid. It was only later that I connected them with the possibility of physical healing.

The only good thing I ever heard about sickness was when a playmate of mine had scarlet fever and her hair grew back in beautiful titian ringlets. I had straight brown hair, and I implored my people to cut it down to the scalp without the prerequisite fever, but nobody would listen. Like any healthy young creature, I supposed health to be a fact of life, like the sun and the moon, and anything less was an insult and a nuisance. In time, I learned two things: that human beings get sick, sometimes desperately sick, and in the Bible they often got well.

But discovering the exact nature of the Bible cures was another matter. The method the Lord used, so far as I could see, was so effortless as to be more baffling than revealing. His language on occasions of healing was ordinary to the point of being humdrum. He said things like "Rise and walk" or "Be whole of thy plague" or "Receive thy sight," and the sick or handicapped people followed these orders . . . if they were orders. All very simple and unuseful. Sometimes he urged people to have faith. Twice, and only twice, he alluded to sin as somehow related to disease, but he did not come out and say so flatly.

How did Jesus heal? Was it through his unrestricted power and authority as a man unlike any other who ever walked the earth? If so, there was little point in studying the process, since there was no way an ordinary mortal could acquire his unique origin.

I could not quite believe that any part of Jesus' ministry was pointless. One day it occurred to me that I might be asking the wrong question. Perhaps the main issue was not how Jesus healed, but why. That sounded so crazy in my own ears that I was jolted into considering it. If one knew why, what relation it had to the Lord's whole purpose, the how might follow spontaneously. Since the very spontaneity of these recoveries was what baffled, even exasperated me, this avenue had possibilities.

I discredit the theory sometimes offered that Jesus healed as a kind of advertising gimmick, like a pitchman displaying samples of greater attractions to be had inside for a price. It is true that he once said, "Except ye see signs and wonders, ye will not believe,"[1] but he may have meant something quite different that I shall discuss later; and sometimes he admonished people to keep a healing quiet. But he does not seem to have been a reluctant healer. He did his work boldly, in the daytime, often outdoors, among onlookers numbering from a few to many hundreds, in the streets and marketplaces, at festivals, in the synagogues. At his trial, he said, "I was daily with you in the temple. . . . I spake openly to the world . . . and in secret have I said nothing."[2]

When a Roman army officer appealed to Jesus to help his ailing servant, the officer did so because he had heard of him that he healed people. This officer was part of an alien occupation force, more decent than many but still not overly cozy with the subjugated populace. He would scarcely have heard of Jesus at all if his deeds were not common knowledge.

In Geoffrey Household's exquisite short story based upon this incident, the Roman captain, while out on patrol a few days before, had actually seen Jesus performing a cure, and he says of it, "I know the power to command when I see it."

Command. That word pinpoints my own interest in the whole subject. As I have said, I was not motivated like a doctor or nurse by a desire to minister to humanity—though obviously I'm not against that—but rather by a deep instinct that autonomy is the major goal of living, full-scale self-achievement. I don't mean an egocentric arrogance, but an unshakeable responsibility for one's own identity and experience. Nor does autonomy imply that human beings can run things—that's God's business—but we can and must command ourselves within the framework of our lives. Sickness debilitates and blocks this full-scale becoming.

Whatever else it is, the Bible is a book about deliverance from bondage in a hundred thousand contexts. As Moses taught the right to freedom from tyranny without, Jesus brought liberty from bondage within. The etymology of *liberty* includes a word meaning "to grow up." There is no genuine freedom without maturity, and lack of it sets loose a long train of evils, from wars to drug addiction. Sickness brings about an infantile dependency that is deadly to growing up and to self-command. Disease is more than hurtful and harassing. It is anti-man.

That is an important reason to link physical well-being with salvation, but I am not saying the Lord thought exactly so. Anyone who professes to know the mind of Jesus, beyond the bare record, is in boggy territory.

In the arts one soon realizes he cannot have final answers. There are only interim answers, which is better anyway because they are living. They live with you and work for you so long as you and the questions they pertain to are on the same plane. When the answers no longer respond, it is because you are no longer putting the questions. You have completed that phase of your craft and moved on to a new one where there are different queries. The old answers have not failed or been negated—quite the opposite. They have done their job and released you to the next stage, more questions, a wider search. It is not different in the area of spiritual learning.

So then, for me, a working answer to why Jesus healed is that bodily ills distract men and women from growing all the way up and frustrate their becoming whatever they have in them to be. Sickness is a kind of half-life, especially when it is prolonged, because sickness of whatever duration concentrates energy upon itself, away from the business of living. And that is evil.

Possibly the most significant contribution of Christianity to the world is the principle of incarnation, the God-with-us that Jesus Christ personified. Unlike the dominant theme in Oriental mysticism of disincarnation, melting the too too solid flesh back into being in order to be at one with it, the Christian doctrine is embodiment of being in individuality, from a crystal to man. Life as we know it may be a metaphor, but it is not a hoax. In whatever condition we find ourselves, we can find God with us, that is the glad news of Christianity. "Whither shall I go from thy spirit? . . . If I make my bed in hell, behold, thou art there. . . ."[3]

A human being is, like the Trinity from which the pattern is derived, a threefold creature of mind, body, and spirit. But this threeness is not divisible into layers or components. Each pervades the whole and the person is one person, a unified being. The body is our third dimension, much as in Elias Canetti's superb image "Flags are wind made visible."[4] We are spirit and mind made flesh, or in third dimensional expression, in the same way—though by no means to the same degree—that Christ Jesus was.

I am indebted to Dr. Paul Tournier for pointing out that when the Bible speaks negatively of "the flesh," it does not mean the body as if it were some despicable part of man. *Flesh* in that sense means the attempt to live without God, without salvation; in other words, a worship of materiality as if it were the all of living. If Jesus came to show us the way out of the flesh, he first shows us the way into it—"a body hast thou prepared me"[5]—by wearing the same material jacket himself and by restoring others' bodies to soundness. His purpose was nothing short of a redefinition of man, with both health and holiness as explicit states of his implicit nature.

It is widely known that *health* and *holiness* are at bottom the same word, *whole.* Various dictionary definitions of both terms overlap with words like *sane, sound, hale, well, wise, whole.* As an arrangement of atoms, a body is a material object like others that will one day disintegrate. But as a statement of individuality by the one who possesses it, a body is an organic structure of ideas. It may well be as much the owner's affair to maintain its wholeness as it is to keep his character intact.

It does not appear to us that either sickness or health is within our control, but suppose they are? And that awakening us to this control or command was a critical ingredient in Christ's viewpoint? How it might have been lost in the first place, or came to be unrecognized, I cannot guess, but the *Christian* treatment of sick people would certainly include what is too often missing in modern medicine—a reverence for the wonder and mystery of being alive, a sense of the sanctity of men and women. Without that, we are healing the torso, not the person.

A friend of mine who supported herself as a medical artist left hospital work when she found the staff never spoke of patients as people, nor even as ailing bodies, but as the disease or malfunctioning organ itself. They were the gall bladder in 704 or the broken leg in 563 or the ulcer in 415. Upon inquiry, my friend was told that this was partly "scientific"; partly a result of numbers (when you got that many sick people under one roof, you had to start cataloging them); and partly a defense against wear and tear on the staff's emotions (if you let yourself care about them, you'd be a wreck). My friend chose to be a humane, if hungry, artist, lest she lose her sensitivity altogether. She had some lean years, but she made it.

The primitive association of medicine with religion may not have been so unsound as modern theories would paint it. The pitfall in it, of course, is superstition—false theology and false doctoring. But the pitfall in coolly technical medicine is its splintered view of the patient. Medical practice that detaches itself from spirit and mind detaches itself from the actual thing that health is and from the energy that heals, or wholes.

In the 1950s I had occasion to interview Brigadier General Rawley E. Chambers, at that time head of the neuropsychiatric division of the United States Army Medical Corps. He was a big white-haired man with a fascinating background. A sergeant in World War I, he had for a time had charge of burial detail on the battlefields, and he kept coming across "bodies" that were not dead but shell-shocked. He grew interested in the human psyche, returned to go to college and medical school, and rose through the ranks of the army to become a general officer. He was so genial and so devoid of jargon that I grew bold enough to remark that he was an unusual psychiatrist.

He replied, "Well, there is a reason for that."

"Do you mind telling me what it is?" I asked.

He turned a paper weight slowly over and over. "I don't believe psychiatry is God," he said. "I thought it was, once, but if it were we would have the answers by now, and we simply don't."

Transplantation of human spare parts; equipment that keeps an otherwise lifeless body functioning metabolically; the shrugging off as trivial risk a 2 percent "bad reaction" to drugs and anesthetics that are beneficial in most cases—a young girl whose father died of a bad reaction said to me that to those who die the risk is 100 percent—all this illustrates the reduction of human beings to machinery. The technique works mechanistically and on percentages, but more and more it leaves humanity floundering. Well-being becomes something done *to* us by an awesome and arcane class, and we feel instinctively that this is somehow wrong.

So do many individual medical men. I heard an English doctor lecture on Chinese acupuncture, which he studied for ten years and later taught. He deplored the tendency of Western medicine to separate people from their complete make-up and said that this was nowhere more apparent than in the attempt to have two kinds of hospitals, one for mental illness and one for physical disease. "What are you going to do?" he asked. "Send the patient's body to one hospital and his mind to another?"

A surgeon in New York once told me he would not so much as remove a sliver from a man's finger unless the man believed he as surgeon could do it. He said he had quite enough work on his hands without having to do the patient's work as well. I heard another doctor say that no system of treatment could of itself restore health. What it did was help persuade the person to assert himself against the disease.

Is that so different from Jesus' injunction to rise and walk? And might not this be more rationally an action of the whole person, willingness and energy included, than of physicality alone? When Jesus told a man with a useless hand to stretch it forth, he was requiring him to do the very thing he could not do. When he said to a deaf man, "Be opened," and to a blind man, "Look up," was he not persuading them to assert themselves, to call upon untapped spiritual energies?

It sounds a little odd to suggest health as a form of worship, but it is at least fresh, and as an explanation for why Jesus concerned himself with it, it is worth considering. I can see no grounds for supposing that integrity of body is any less important to the Creator of whole man than integrity of mind, or what some would call sinlessness. Jesus may have been reminding us that it is only part-knowledge to know God. We must know that we know and act on what we know, and this, Jesus said, would make us free.

I think that most of my superiors in religion would agree that life in God is understood not through reason or doctrine but through experience, and the body is that dimension of ourselves that we experience most directly and soonest. A baby playing with its toes is finding out that it has a body of interest and importance. What it finds out with is mind and spirit, but it takes much longer to be consciously aware of these. We can think long before we can think about thinking, and it is possible to go through life employing our minds and spirits without ever regarding them objectively.

In finding our God-life, we begin not with instruction but with events. The Buddhists know this and their teaching, to our Western mentalities, goes backwards. They provide instruction only after the learner has acquired some experience with Buddhist practice, and by then often he doesn't need it. A friend of mine took the Zen course in archery and found it extremely frustrating. He was given no rules or theory; he just went out day after day with a master at his side and shot the arrow. He was not good at it, and this irritated and embarrassed him. If they would just tell him what he was supposed to be doing, perhaps he could do it a little better. But that was just the point: they expressly wanted him not to pursue something laid down or decreed by others as proper, but to discover in himself both his own capacity and the laws of archery. It might or might not be what others did. Who were they to dictate that? He did not yet know this, but the breakthrough, when it came, was like a sudden release from a cocoon, and it altered his entire sense of himself.

It seems likely to me that Jesus was doing something similar by healing. In that sense, he may well have used the healings, as the Zen Buddhists use archery, to call attention to the range of God-living, but never as a mere come-on to be dropped as soon as the deeper meanings were perceived. He once prayed for others, not that God would remove them from the world, as if to be here at all was shameful, "but that thou shouldest keep them from evil."[6]

We have no evidence that Jesus regarded the world as a travesty. The world was his home, so much so that he was tied down to no residence. He was at home in the desert and mountains, in palaces and fishermen's shacks, because he was at home in himself. He spoke with power and love of the living world of ordinary men and women—of building and plowing, of cooking and fishing, of planting and harvest; of wine and oil, salt and bread, wildflowers and herbs; of books and babies, honeycombs and fig trees, weather and weddings, journeys and homecomings; of candlelight and corn, shoes and hens, vineyards, markets, treasures, sheepfolds, doorways.

He was far from other-worldly in the usual sense, and he said his purpose was "not to condemn the world; but that through him the world might be saved."[7] He assured people that God loved the world, and announced more than once that he had no intention of destroying it.

One summer many years ago my husband and I

lived in a driftwood cabin on the northernmost rim of Cape Cod. The sun rose and set in water—from the Atlantic on our right and into Massachusetts Bay on the northwest. I liked to get up at dawn and walk along the water's edge to see this daily miracle of the sun emerging from the sea. During the night the surf had obliterated all tracks, even those of animals and birds, so that I walked there as if I were the first creature alive.

As the sun rose, dripping and gigantic, from the vast horizon, I faced directly into it, and I felt with the impact of personal discovery that the sun was still, the earth in motion. Of course I already knew that in my head, but in that moment it became tangibly real to me. I literally felt the earth rolling majestically, taking me with it. I was both onlooker and participant, within and without. I did not cause what was happening, but it was my event. It was happening for half a billion people too, but that was half a billion other events. The nearest way I can explain it is to say that it was like recovery after a long illness, that delicious sense of coming back to one's proper self. It was at once awesome and perfectly natural. I was divided between stunned silence and cavorting about like some demented creature, "walking, and leaping, and praising God."[8]

Jesus commanded his environment as a bird commands the air which is its native habitat, or a fish the sea, and he intimated that such was our heritage, too. Health was part and parcel of his world-view. Healing that integrates the individual's body with mind and spirit at the same time invariably integrates the person with the creation that is his domain. How could there be dominion over all the earth that left out command of our own bodies, which are part of the earth?

If we seek to know why Jesus healed, we have also to ask why anybody else does. Why does a man become a doctor, or a mother tend an ailing child? That may seem obvious, but upon reflection it discloses belief in a correlation between life and goodness, a belief so deep it astonishes us to have it mentioned. Back of all attempts to heal is an assumption, however unspecified and general, that health is natural, desirable, and attainable—or ought to be, and what is *ought* except a moral issue? When life seems to us not good, something is wrong and we know it's wrong. Most people, if asked, would probably say life is a mixture of good and bad, but unless they thought the good was somehow more authentic, they would not likely make an effort to change the bad, to stop being poor or maltreated or sick. No one, when he is perfectly well, tries to get a disease on the grounds that disease too is part of living and one must expect to have both states. There must be an underlying conviction that health is a right and disease an infringement that we have authority to resist. If the Lord was concerned with teaching humanity its moral rights, health could easily have been one of them.

Again, to ask why Jesus healed involves us in asking why people want to be healed. Anyone in his right mind would rather be comfortable than miserable. But Jesus healed to a purpose, never to a vacuum.

He said repeatedly to those he restored, "Go thy way," "Go into thine house," "Go home to thy friends." What did he mean if not that they were to get busy with their lives, to go on with whatever was their particular journey before it was interrupted by disability? When he cured Peter's mother-in-law of a fever, she promptly got up and served food and performed other housewifely tasks, which were her accustomed work.

It is not selfish or reprehensible to be healthy, but it is to be lazy, greedy, or indifferent. The question hanging over anyone seeking health is what he wants it for. What will he do with it once he has got it? This is not a moral question—or anyway not only that—but a fiercely practical one. I have seen a zoo animal released to freedom yet still pacing a nonexistent cage. Habit was stronger than iron bars until the animal was led by a keeper past the old limits. Then it learned to be an animal again, not a caged thing. Capacities must be realized in action, or the result is paralyzing. All that Jesus did was designed to lead humanity out of mistaken inhibition.

I have become more and more convinced that Jesus healed people because it was the most vivid and immediate means he had of giving firsthand experience in his dominant thesis, the correlation of earth and heaven. To him, these were never at variance, and the body is each one's first universe. Every person of whatever age, sex, race, class, or education has a body that matters to him, that is capable of being hurt or impaired. To restore it physically by spiritual means unites earth and heaven in an intimate and unmistakable way. Healing touches everyone at his most vulnerable point, as well as that area that each has in common with everyone else. No one is immune by reason of status. And no one, great or humble, who went from pain, indignity, and despair to freedom and function under the Lord's touch would ever again imagine heaven to be a remote and thinly "spiritual" realm.

This is a great evil, the alienation of our ordinary lives from divinity, the idea that earth is one thing and heaven another. In the beginning they were a correlated unit. "In the beginning," the record says, "God created the heaven and the earth,"[9] together, in the same act, and nowhere are they set against one another. There is no dividing line between our manifested human lives and the absolute of which they are the concretion.

The alleged antagonism between spirit and flesh, the one presumably pure, the other corrupt, is very old. In the second century, Tertullian was already writing of it as a long-held delusion and expounding the premise that Jesus of Nazareth reunited them in healing and most gloriously by his own resurrection. Tertullian translates the word *incorrupt* where it appears in the New Testament as *unimpaired.*

When after his return from burial the Lord sought to convince the disciples that he was real, not an apparition, he not only offered a body that they could touch, but also one that functioned as theirs did—he ate fish and honeycomb before them. The body is our instrument, much as a violin or a piano is a musician's instrument, without which the music in us would be silenced.

In the Masoretic text of the Old Testament, translated by Jewish scholars into English, the word *perfect* when applied to people is *wholehearted.* An object or an animal may be perfect, but a person is wholehearted. "Thou shalt be wholehearted with the Lord thy God."[10] "The upright shall dwell in the land, and the wholehearted shall remain in it."[11] The great Israeli thinker Martin Buber built almost his entire philosophy on this wholeness of heart. Modern man, Buber said, is fragmented, not wholly alive, willing, open, or compassionate, because he fancies that his day-to-day existence is separate from if not actually antagonistic to divine values. This wrecks his nature and decentralizes it, so that he does not know himself, love himself, have himself. To an even lesser extent can he find wholeness in others, or give it. Buber believed, and I agree, that wholeness is possible only as an outcome of known oneness with the Eternal Thou, what Christians call Father or God. Only then does human life take on the glow of being actual.

Wholehearted. It has a musical sound, like bells at evening, a purity and lightness of spirit so conscious that even in conflict there would be no hatred. *Wholehearted* connotes a nexus so total that evil could in no guise shatter or dissolve it. In sickness this would heal, and in death there would be no discontinuity. Something of that kind is, for me, the why of Christ's healing.

But we still need to know how.

2 how was it done? faith

SOMEONE IS BOUND TO ASK WHETHER I myself have had a physical healing by spiritual means alone. Yes, I have. And some of these occasions I shall refer to elsewhere, but don't look for a detailed narrative account. In the first place, I doubt that case histories prove very much. There is no way one person's experience can be made a norm for others. Healing, whether medically or spiritually induced, is a highly private affair. Nobody has lived precisely what I have lived up to now, nor thought my thoughts, and therefore no one could reproduce exactly my circumstances, even if he wanted to—nor could I take over his. Any doctor will tell you that treatment effective for one person can be useless or even harmful to another.

In the second place, any attempt to recount in orderly sequence just what occurred at once falsifies it. Spiritual healing is not accomplished by traditional logic, and the effort to reconstruct it along these lines gives a wrong idea. That is why Jesus so often spoke in parables. *Parable* means a kind of running-along-beside. It is a sort of elongated metaphor wherein one thing is stated to convey another that cannot be stated. I recognize the yen for an explanation, and I have tried within minutes of its happening to write down what actually took place in a given healing, but it always evaporates in my hands—not the healing itself, but the explanation.

This does not mean we ought not to talk of these things at all, or that spiritual healing must remain obscure and chancy. It means that words must not substitute for the spirit. Words can at most bear witness to the event; they do not create or constitute it. It is a little like trying to explain how you came to fall unaccountably in love when it is just that—unaccountable.

Jesus once restored the sight of a man who was born blind. Skeptics who had known the man all his life badgered him with arguments as to why it could not possibly have happened as it did. It was a trick, or his parents had done something, or God touched him mystically. Over and over the man described what the Lord had done, but they would not have it that way. At last, the exasperated man said that he could not cope with their sophisticated debate, "but one thing I know, that, whereas I was blind, now I see."[1] Healings are lived and felt, not represented.

A third reason I distrust case histories is that they too easily come between a seeker and his own experience, so that he fails to see his own way, and that is the very worst thing I could do. I remember once in my early years imploring an established writer to tell me how she worked, how many hours or pages per day, whether she kept a notebook, that sort of thing. She replied, "What makes me a writer will never in a thousand years make you one. Finding your own technique is part of the job. If I told you what I do, it might console you, but it will not help you."

That was courtesy of a high order. I did not have a thousand years to waste. A fatter ego might have enjoyed having me trail around as an acolyte, but she told me a basic truth and credited me with the good sense to use it. By that much, I got on with my own work sooner, and I remain in her debt.

Healing is an art, even as writing is, a subtle blend of character, skill, and experience, no exact duplicate of which can ever exist in any two people. To suggest that it can be manufactured from borrowed experience is like claiming you, too, can be a Rembrandt by filling in colors on those numbered canvases to be had in variety stores—yellow on six, brown on seven, scarlet on ten.

There is an old Jewish legend about one Rabbi Zusya who as he lay dying said, "In the world to come I shall not be asked, 'Why were you not Moses?' but 'Why were you not Zusya?' " To become wholly oneself, which is what life is all about, is to be whole in oneself, which is healing, and it can only be done singly. For me to offer my own events as blueprints would be presumptuous. All I can truly say from my own encounter with it is that spiritual healing does occur and is genuine. One does not have to be a moral genius, but the effort must be made from the depths of the personality.

Fourth and last, no one should be influenced by my procedure, because I am not good enough at it. I am too slow and make too many uncertain moves. That I succeed at all is by God's good grace or else a kind of trial-and-error inevitability. When one is ill, it is no laughing matter to himself, but I have sometimes imagined the Lord good-naturedly plucking me out of puddles and thickets into which I blunder by doing all the wrong things, brushing me off, and setting me on my feet—and it makes me smile. Laughter is not a bad healing agent. It puts a distance between oneself and the conceit of the disease, and that is one of the ways, I find, that healing is accomplished, a letting go of intensity. Until it happens, one scarcely realizes how tenaciously he clutches the very thing he is trying to get rid of.

So far as I know, Jesus did not use laughter to heal (although he showed flashes of humor in his teaching), but in Proverbs it is written, "A merry heart doeth good like a medicine."[2] In Hebrew it is even more direct: "A merry heart is a good medicine."

Christian healing is determinately different from medical practice, different not in degree but in kind. But healing is healing, is it not? From the standpoint of physical function, yes. From the standpoint of self-realization, no. Therapeutics searches for a cause and removes it; metaphysics seeks to gain a fresh view which in turn alters the appearance. Moreover, it liberates the person, which, as I have said, means to grow up. One gets on with becoming oneself.

Jesus healed people by causing them to see themselves in the light that he threw upon them. This was not merely an alternative form of treatment; it was a different evaluation of what was going on—what life is, what humanity is, what disease and health are, how things work. That is why and how his theology entered into it. Jesus' concept of God-and-man as entity underlay and was a precondition to all that he did.

Spiritual healing is neither psychosomatic nor miraculous in the ordinary sense of infracting natural law. Jesus did not violate law, he advanced it. A man sending radio or television messages with no connecting wire to carry them is no less phenomenal than one walking on water, but neither of them is defying law; they are both utilizing it. When Jesus walked on the sea, he did not cancel out gravity, or he would have gone off into space. He tamed gravity and utilized it.

Other people use gravity in unique ways. Early in my career, I moved into a New York apartment that was three flights up in a remodeled brownstone building. I did not own much furniture, but some of it was heavy, and there were big boxes of books. The moving men carried all of it on their backs, with long strips of gray cloth binding each load across their chests or foreheads. I noticed that they would pause before every stage, when they hoisted the load from the truck, again before the apartment house door, and at the bottom of each flight of stairs.

Concerned, I finally asked one of them, "Is it too heavy? What are you waiting for?"

"Gravity," he said, and he meant it. "I'm waitin' for the world to move. You gotta go with the spin and then you can lift anything."

That man might have been surprised to hear he was teaching me something about the works of Jesus Christ, but he was. Jesus said a mustard seed's worth of faith could move mountains; why not a gram of gravity to pick up a chest of drawers? Any baseball player knows that when he is leaning away from the direction the ball is traveling, it is very tricky to realign his body forces to make a smooth play, but with even a slight inclination toward the trajectory, he can be brilliant.

The Lord made wine out of water but not out of thin air. He fed five thousand people with five loaves of bread and a couple of fish, but not with nothing. When he came out of his own tomb, he did not suddenly materialize outside of it but removed the stone that sealed his cave and emerged like any other man, leaving the linen graveclothes neatly folded behind him. I am not inferring limits on Jesus' power—we know that he did appear in a closed room a little later—but he was ever conscious of pointing the way for us, and there may be a vital factor here concerning healing. Perhaps we are not to look for miracles outrageous to common sense, but to build upon and expand that which already is and we already know. That at least would be one way to begin, a place to start. Spiritual healing is a reinterpretation of the facts.

It might be well to point out a distinction between healing and being healed, though they are interwoven like the warp and woof of a fabric. The Lord certainly rescued himself from difficulties on several occasions, but only on the cross and in the tomb did he do what most of us are trying to do: heal ourselves. There is nothing sinister in this desire. Ideally, one would use an understanding of Christian healing to aid others, even as one might teach another to read, but you would not get far if you yourself could not read. And teaching yourself is a slightly different matter. So, too, being one's own patient means learning the tasks of both the healer and the healed. Though they form one whole piece of cloth or end result, they have somewhat different functions.

It is known that Jesus healed by faith, but it is often overlooked that that faith was in the petitioners, not in himself. He had no need of faith; he *knew.* "When Jesus then lifted up his eyes and saw a great company of people come unto him, he saith unto Philip, Whence shall we buy bread, that these may eat? And this he said to prove him: for he himself knew what he would do."[3]

Outside the tomb of Lazarus, the Lord thanked God aloud for hearing him, then promptly half-apologized. Between his Father and himself such explicitness was absurd, but for the people's sake he spoke, that their belief in God's power might be deepened.

During a tugboat strike in New York harbor, the

captain of an ocean liner decided to dock his huge vessel unassisted. Up to that time, this had not been tried, and at the best of times, it takes enormous skill. A split-second's miscalculation, and 92 million pounds of steamship would slice right through a pier and halfway into the city street. It had to be done in slack water, at the turning of the tide, for otherwise the currents were unmanageable. Besides that, there were over two thousand lives at stake.

The captain stood on the bridge, calling orders to his engine room, and laid the great ship alongside the pier as gently as an elephant cracking an egg. Just before they came to a stop, the executive officer glanced at his skipper's face and gasped, "Why, you're enjoying this!" The captain said later he knew it could be done because he had had to do it on Navy ships in wartime.

The difference between the healer and the healed is something like that. That ship's crew had enough faith in their skipper to obey his orders, and between them they executed a small—or maybe not so small—miracle. Like the ship captain, Jesus knew, because he had worked it out alone with God in the wilderness, at the beginning of his career. We need faith—until such time as we too have worked our way to full knowledge.

Faith is the patient's contribution to the transaction. But suppose one hasn't got it—or hasn't got enough, anyway. The Lord once asked the father of an epileptic boy to believe, and the father replied in anguish—the Bible says "with tears"—"Lord, I believe; help thou mine unbelief."[4] It has a familiar ring. We too would believe, if we only knew how. I am quite sure nobody knows how at the outset. People who have faith work for it; it is not just handed to anyone.

Sometimes I make speeches to students or others who feel they would like to be writers. Often they think that, because I earn my living writing, I must always know precisely what I am doing. It is not so. One knows a little, sometimes painfully little, and accepts the burden of learning the rest. Some of my listeners don't like that much, preferring the easy dream of sudden glory to the discipline of learning a craft. Anybody could do that. Exactly. Note that *discipline* and *disciple* are at bottom the same word, and it means "to learn."

Faith is a learned thing, and to complain of not having it is like complaining of not knowing how to walk. You were born to go upright, but the skill must be acquired on your own two feet and through taking your own spills. There is no way others can learn to walk for you. They can provide two aids only: encouragement and example.

A woman I was trying to acquaint with prayer said to me, "I *wish* I could believe!" and I replied, "No, you wish you believed more. You already believe something or you wouldn't be holding this conversation with me. It may be a mustard seed, but you've got it, and that's enough to start with. The Lord said so."

It is genuine and workable to seek more faith, because that is how it grows, and one of the ways that we grow, too. Even the disciples said, "Lord, increase our faith."[5] It is not genuine to insist you have no faith at all. For one thing, it's trying to find a short cut and that won't wash in this business of healing. To go in one leap from nothing to something is indeed a full-blown miracle, the work of the skilled craftsman. Would you expect to begin at the top? Moreover, the plea of no faith is hedging your bets. It means, "If nothing comes of this endeavor, I shall not look like a fool, because I didn't believe in the first place, and I said so."

Worst of all, the loud proclamation that one has no faith is daring God: "Do something wonderful and I shall have all the faith you like." This, I think, is why Jesus groaned, "Except ye see signs and wonders, ye will not believe."[6] Faith that is proved is no faith at all; it is knowledge, experience, wisdom—all kinds of other things. Faith is always in advance of the fact. "What a man seeth, why doth he yet hope for?"[7]

Faith, then, is impossible. Of course. That is why it accomplishes the impossible. Long before Jesus' day, God ordered the Israelites to cross the river Jordan when they had no boats, bridge, or any means at all. They formed into ranks and marched off, forty thousand armed men plus all the families and animals and household goods. They must have felt rather foolish. Not until the leaders' feet were actually in the water did the river divide and open a pathway through. The faith Jesus asked of people, or sometimes commended them for, was not merely saying they believed, nor willingness to be persuaded, nor even blind hope in his extraordinary power. It was more nearly an acceptance of the impossible. That isn't easy; nobody claims that it is.

And yet there is no living person to whom this acceptance is beyond reach because, to stay alive from one sunrise to the next, we employ faith constantly. It is native stuff. We lie down to sleep with no guarantee that the world will be there when we wake up. On the highway we follow road signs at seventy miles an hour, believing they will not bring disaster. At the lowest ebb, a man who commits suicide does it believing that there is an answer somehow better than the one he has—oblivion or a new start, whichever he thinks awaits him. We believe in many kinds of order so spontaneously that we don't even know it is belief and imagine that it is all proven and factual.

Asking how to believe and not receiving a direct answer is frustrating, but the reason is that there never are exact answers in any creative endeavor, and healing is creativity in the highest degree. What makes the arts creative is that nobody has been there before you, and the how of your special gift doesn't exist until you live it into reality. The same is true of faith and healing.

People ask me often how to write or, more broadly, how to use their talents—in short, how to be creative. I could say that only when they stop asking how and start doing it any old way that they can, will they have the answer to their question, but that's cold-hearted and backward, anyway. I respect the yearning because it has motivated half my life, and they will come to their own letting go of craving to know how when they have groped their way, as we all do, to the first faint self-realization, which is what they are really after.

In simple courtesy, if not in Christian charity, I can hold out a hand to them, as I would to an infant who finds himself anchored to a spinning earth by the soles of his two small feet and thinks, "What next?" Such hands were held out to me in my search for creativity, believe me, and in my journey to religious discovery. Nobody learns these things in splendid isolation.

Here, then, are a few rules of thumb—they are no more than that. They are not meant to be faith in ten easy lessons, nor even to be taken sequentially. They are more like tools that I fashioned as I went along. Somewhere you may recognize one that can be bent to your own purposes, and that is the one for you to start with.

1. Accept if you can the premise that there aren't any rules in the ordinary sense. Faith isn't a technique, it's a personal adventure—as personal as a love affair.

2. Try to notice the faith you already live with daily. I find it in writing because that is the work I know best, but I also find it in cooking, gardening, walking on the beach, and just about everything else. When I sit down to write, I am surrounded by a sea of notes, interviews, clippings, ideas, but I have no exact knowledge of how it is all going together. Sometimes I don't even know where to begin. In order not to sit staring at blank paper forever, I select an idea or a fact that interests me and write it down. It may lead no-

where, so I choose another. Sooner or later, a second sentence evolves out of the first, and I am under way. If I waited until the pattern was clearly in my head, I would wait forever, frozen into inaction.

The Lord often taught by parables. Learning to see the faith you use in ordinary tasks is living your own parables. Reflect on them. See what they have to say about faith in general.

3. Utilize this commonplace faith in religious directions, and start small. Try healing a kitchen cut on your finger, or curing a common cold (not so small, that), or banishing a headache. Don't confront a sycamore tree and order it into the nearest lake.

A beginner in this business of faith told me that the dividing of the Red Sea was the last thing she could ever accept. I said she wasn't required to begin at the end, and we spoke of starting small. She was a middle-aged woman reentering the labor force and eager to make good in her first job. One day her new boss sent her on an errand that took rather longer than either of them expected, and when she started back it was raining in torrents. She had no protection, not even a coat, and she could ill afford to ruin her clothing.

Huddling in the entry to a bank, she thought, half in anger, half-amused, "All right, Lord, you divided the Red Sea, I guess. Can't you dry up a rainstorm for a few minutes?" At that moment, a man came out of the bank with an enormous black umbrella, sized up her situation, and offered to escort her wherever she was going. As soon as she could after returning, she phoned me and fairly shouted, "*Of course* he opened the Red Sea! Why didn't you say so?" But she had said it for herself now, and it was part of her. Start small and you may get a bigger answer than you expect, but it will always be one you can use.

4. Go beyond where you have been before. One reason faith often works in a crisis is that, when the chips are down, people spontaneously push back the previous boundaries of belief. They stop limiting their possibilities and give faith elbow room.

For many years I worked for an editor who drove me wild when he ordered a rewrite by saying airily, "I don't care what you do to it, just make it wonderful." I had two choices: I could quit or I could make a stab at it. Gradually, I learned that he could not tell me how to follow his instruction because he didn't know. The story existed in my head and sensibilities, not his. He was a good editor precisely because he had the sense and the audacity to exact from me, or any writer, what I was too drained at the moment to require of myself—that last extra impossible effort. He forced me to live up to my capacity and a shade beyond; to do more when I had already done everything; to cast my net, like Peter, one more time than I thought rational. And slowly I grew into what I most wanted to become, a writer.

I doubt very much that Jesus had any intention of thinking for us. When a man asked him to intervene in a family quarrel, he replied, "Who made me a judge or a divider over you?"[8] A scribe sought to have him name the greatest commandment, and Jesus, good teacher that he was, at once turned the question back upon him. "What is written in the law? How readest thou?"[9] This was pure Socratic method: I will not answer your question, but I will show you that you can answer it yourself, and by this you shall begin to find out who you are. Faith is the resources we haven't dared to explore, much less use, until someone or some event demands it.

5. Don't try to use faith to avoid the rough work of thinking—it blurs and spoils both powers. Faith is not antagonistic to reason; it is a perfectly respectable alternative means of discovering and working with the laws of being. Faith is in disrepute partly because it looks on the surface much easier than what Percy Bridgman, Nobel physicist, once called "doing one's damnedest with one's mind, no holds barred." This was Bridgman's definition of scientific method. Faith could be said to be doing one's damnedest with one's spirit, no holds barred.

The faith required to be healed is always according to one's character. "Unto whomsoever much is given, of him shall be much required,"[10] so that the faith that suffices for one could be negligible in another. Faith is available to the most sophisticated intellect, and reason is available to any honest heart in its degree. I have seen a mentally retarded adult, once he believed it was possible, use and develop his own reasoning ability in a manner that, on a different mental plane, would be called brilliant.

To say that Jesus spurned intellect is just not true. At the age of twelve, he took on the temple scholars in a dialectic that staggered them. With Nicodemus, a member of Sanhedrin, the supreme tribunal of the Jews, he held a recondite discussion far into the night. But he did not exclude humble minds from this kind of thing, if they had curiosity. At Jacob's well Jesus talked philosophy with a village woman, to the bewilderment of his companions. She was not only a woman and therefore a simpleton, but a despicable Samaritan, too. Had their master lost track of the proprieties? "His disciples . . . marvelled that he talked with the woman: yet no man said, What seekest thou? or, Why talkest thou with her?"[11]

It is the divorce of faith from intellect that makes them both sometimes evil—as with the Nazis and cold reason, for example, or the Inquisition and rabid faith. Without the mind, we could have no faith at all, as an idea or a word—at most it would be the sort of blind trust a dog has in a man. While without countless spiritual factors like courage, zest, belief in truth, the exercise of mind wouldn't last a week. The greatest possible faith will not write my manuscripts, yet no amount of intellect can make me brave or compassionate—I could fake it, but I would not be it. To discern when and when not faith or intellect is the requisite temper takes experience, but to know that one does not supplant the other is a long step in acquiring the faith that heals and that sometimes seems elusive.

Faith and fear are incompatible. You may swing back and forth between the two, but you cannot really feel both simultaneously. I once interviewed a Dutch woman who had escaped from the Nazis by walking over the Pyrenees mountains, with a six-year-old child in tow. She said that the main thing she learned was that fear is always in the future. Even when what is happening is painful or abominable, you do not fear it. You fear that it will get worse, or that you may not acquit yourself well, but you are never afraid of the present. She said that from this basis she was able to dispel the child's fear and cope with her own.

Also, she found that it took energy to fear, and attention, both of which she needed constantly for more important matters: to watch her footing so that falling rocks or snapping twigs did not catch the ears of the border patrol; to breathe properly; to rest without sleeping; to soothe the child so that she did not whimper, and so on. No doubt, she said, she would be afraid again someday, but she would never fear fear itself, for she knew what it was now, a kind of nothingness up ahead that drained strength and created its own conditions.

Fear works against healing in much the same way. It concentrates one's powers away from the ameliorative forces that would build and save. Fear tenses the whole body and hampers its workings, as doctors know well. Faith is more than hope; it is the antidote to fear and has an actual physical effect. That's one reason faith is worth cultivating in good times, so that you have it in reserve when you need it.

Faith is a total acceding of the personality to the power that causes it. Christ Jesus displayed such faith on the cross when he said, "Into thy hands I commend my spirit."[12] Job acknowledged it in his saying, "Even though he slay me, yet will I trust in him."[13] Esther the Queen attained it when she flouted the king's edict for the sake of a moral point, and said, "If I perish, I perish."[14]

We are not pushed to such extremes as a rule, but the *quality* of holy faith is the same in all gradations. A long time ago when I was first inquiring into the nature of spiritual healing, I went by train from New York to Philadelphia to do a magazine interview. I was nursing a heavy cold, and it would have been a courtesy to cancel the interview, but we were faced with a deadline, and the professor I was to see had opted for going through with it.

During most of the two-hour trip, I prayed and pondered, but there was no abatement of the symptoms. I was simply streaming, and armed with a large box of tissues. About thirty minutes before arriving, I gave up, thinking something like this, "All right, Lord, if this is the way you want me to go into that man's office, I don't understand it, but I'll do it," and I turned my attention to the job before me. As I sat down across the desk from the professor, he grinned and asked, "Are you planning to mop up the floor with me?" I looked at the box of tissues amazed. The cold had vanished, I didn't know when. Keeping my mind on that interview was a struggle, I was much too taken up with the healing.

On the way home, I wrote down all I could remember concerning it, mostly in the form of questions. Was this faith? Did God somehow want me to give up, and was that what triggered the result? If I had given up at the beginning, would it have cured me sooner, and if so, would it have been better not to pray at all? Surely not. People went to Jesus constantly in search of healing, and he never once turned anyone down, though in his hometown, "he did not many mighty works there because of their unbelief."[15] Still, even at Nazareth he healed a few, so maybe the mighty works he refrained from were a different sort. The Lord steadily encouraged people to ask, seek, knock, pray, petition. Why, then, aren't the answers swifter, clearer, more sure? Unless spiritual healing is mere caprice on God's part, which seems mad, there must be laws concerning it. Can we know what these laws are, or is that presuming upon God's territory?

Many questions, few answers. But we must honor the questions that arise in us; they are a very special way God talks to us, and if one pays attention, they always lead somewhere that we are trying to go. In my case, such questions brought the recognition that healing was not subject to analysis, and this is fundamental, the launching pad into an intelligible journey along the way of healing. It ought not to seem entirely strange. After all, one cannot fathom poetry by analysis, or music, or great concepts like justice, courtesy, patriotism.

The individual who demands that I tell him exactly what to do to make his story salable, and will not abide the truth that I do not know—because writing is not that kind of clockwork transaction—is very like the one who insists upon a prescription for spiritual healing. Or for acquiring faith. Or for falling in love. I think that is another reason Jesus deplored a petty bargaining for signs and wonders, and not that healing itself is in any way second-rate.

I asked a writer friend how he had managed to write a particularly brilliant magazine article, and he grinned. "With a little talent and a lot of unmitigated nerve," he replied, meaning of course that he couldn't really tell me. An editor once put the same question to me, and I heard myself saying, "I don't wholly know, and I don't want to know. It gets difficult if you look at it too closely."

Being able to analyze faith doesn't bring us one step closer to having it. Faith begins in action, in living out one small event as if you had faith already. Am I saying that faith is another name for courage? I suppose I am. Many of us would like to have more courage, but we don't expect it to rain on us out of blue heaven. We take it as granted that we have a little courage—even the most timid person dares something—and that it expands only as it is used. It is not different with faith. It becomes real and vivid only as we allow it, test it, work, try, risk, commit ourselves, fling ourselves at last into a venture that may sweep us away.

This apparent disruption of logical sequence—moving from action back to understanding—seems to me to be God's way. Therefore, I have no choice but to accept it, trust it, and try to assimilate the new way of thinking. It isn't easy because he speaks only heaven and I speak only earth, but there are ways around language barriers. For one thing, there is faith. For another, there is sign language. Signs? Is healing itself a language, then? Have small healings gone on all the time that I failed to heed or recognize?

This was new country, and I walked softly. I was scared and happy and very excited.

3 how was it done? virtue

AT THE BEGINNING I SAID THAT ONLY A few big ideas take up residence in any one mind over a lifetime. One of my life-shaping ideas was the realization that I didn't have to be perfect. My home training was a curious mix of puritan strictness and free-wheeling flexibility—which I suppose characterized a lot of households in the mid-twentieth century. Perfection in some areas was an absolute standard—in manners, dress, speech, silence, school reports, and so on. When I learned, chiefly through my secular education, that perfection was neither attainable nor entirely desirable, I joined the human race. I became a better friend to myself and to others.

One sparkling facet of this recognition shone upon my researches into spiritual healing: I saw that healing was not something earned. One did not have to be faultless to merit health, nor, on the other hand, was sickness any proof of wrongdoing. One of the great blessings of Christianity as I read it is the doctrine that disease is totally random, therefore totally unjust. If it were in any way justifiable as due punishment for sin, we should have no business tampering with it. This brought a quite new consciousness into the world.

Yet the Bible states unequivocally that virtue was a feature of Jesus' healings. Here again, a switch is inadvertently made, as in the case of faith, but this time in the opposite direction. The mistake is thinking that the virtue was required in the petitioner, while instead it was in the Lord. When a woman in a crowd clandestinely touched his robe, seeking cure, Jesus at once said, "I perceive that virtue is gone out of me."[1] Jesus was beyond question a supremely good man, but how could that heal? In the ordinary sense—that is, if virtue is only piety and decency—it cannot. Something far greater is involved here.

A noticeable fact of the Bible is that its heroes are by and large an unsavory lot—liars, thieves, marauders, cowards, murderers, prostitutes, adulterers, traitors—some of them even turning up in the ancestry of Jesus of Nazareth. Good people sometimes despair over this, asking of what use it is to try to do right; and bad people sometimes seize on it as exculpation for doing whatever they wish. Both positions miss the point, which is openly stated—namely, that God looks upon the heart. We read this but we do not really hear it because we are welded to a cause-and-effect way of thinking. *The heart* to us means our motives and desires, while to God it is the secret core of our being, the center that is not wicked but in some measure unknown even to ourselves, and therefore uninformed, unwise. Jesus said this core was like the wind, "and thou hearest the sound thereof, but canst not tell whence it cometh, and whither it goeth."[2] The things of the spirit are neither understood nor attained by cause-and-effect which is, after all, a technique derived from physics. How then should it form a basis for metaphysics?

We have a passion for explanation at any price and would capture a sunbeam in a box. One of my favorite stories about Einstein is undoubtedly apocryphal, but the point it makes is valid. Einstein had no patience with people who would impose scientific dogma everywhere, and he is alleged to have said, "Breakfast comes before lunch, but breakfast, alas, does not cause lunch." The attempt to make God make sense in ways that we should find compatible is just about as foolish.

Some of the Bible's great people were honorable men and women, too, and if the rogues outnumber them, it is partly because they offer no plausible basis for concluding that God's grace is a reward for proper behavior. "My thoughts are not your thoughts, neither are my ways your ways, saith the Lord."[3] It couldn't be much plainer.

I know an enormously rich industrialist who is a self-made man and a wittily honest one. He says that at times the temptation is almost overwhelming to think, "I make all this money, I *must* be smart." But that temptation knows no class. In a women's prison where I once taught, my students didn't like my saying that I, like them, wondered who I was, where I was going, what should be done with my abilities and my sorrows. To them, "outsiders" were people who pretended to have all the answers, and they felt themselves to be superior because they could see through the pretension. This was understandable. Prisoners have few areas where they can lay claim to superiority, which is a basic human need. But self-righteousness is a parasite wherever it grows. If it is not severely pruned, it takes over and smothers its host.

It is hard for human beings to think straight about sin and virtue—we are too intimately involved, eager to appear in a good light ourselves, and doubtful that there is enough virtue to go around. Why it seldom occurs there is not enough sin to go around, I do not know. In any case, the impulse to exonerate ourselves dates back at least to the book of Job, which some scholars believe is the oldest in the Bible. When Job's friends urged him to confess secret sins—they had to be secret because his visible life was exemplary—that would account for his loss of health, family, property, he refused and accused them of trying to appear virtuous at his expense.

There is a theory about comedy somewhat akin to this explication of tragedy. We really do not know why man laughs. Some claim it is rooted in primitive beliefs that the gods afflicted human beings out of anger or for sport. If someone fell ill or broke a leg, others made fun of him to disguise their terror. Laughter was a kind of camouflage whereby they hoped to escape notice as mere mortals themselves, liable to a similar fate.

Thus, the fun to be found in custard pies, banana peels, and what clowns call "the pain bit"—a hand caught in a mousetrap or a folding chair—echoes the feigned derision of our forebears in the face of real injuries, against which they were otherwise helpless.

It could be true, and it runs parallel to the penchant for attributing sickness to sin, especially other people's sickness. If the victim has sinned and the critic has not, or thinks he hasn't anyway, the critic fabricates a little island of safety for himself. Even Jesus' disciples asked about the man born blind, "Who did sin, this man or his parents?"[4] They too wanted a "rational" explanation. The Lord did not say any of them was totally faultless; what he did say was that sin was not relevant. The blind man's existence, like any other man's, was for the glory of God, and Jesus illustrated this by restoring his sight.

But if healthy and holy are really the same word, does it not follow that well people are holier than sick ones? To my mind, no. That would reduce Christianity to just one more system of rewards-and-punishments, of which the world has always had too many. I doubt that God has a bourgeois mentality. Christianity is a fresh statement of human nature, with both health and sinlessness as part of the inherent structure, like two halves of a walnut, interlinked but not causal of one another.

For ten years of my childhood there was a man in my life who was a storybook father to his children and, since I had no father of my own, to me. He taught me not only what any male parent teaches his girl child—how to dance, wear clothes, be a woman—but also what showmanship is; how to survive in the wilderness; to read biography and history; to move freely in varied cultures—Chinese, Mexican, Indian, among cowhands and fishermen. It is a special kind of blessedness to grow up around an adult like that.

Then it was discovered that he was an embezzler and an arsonist, and it shocked the community. I was about fourteen, and I walked the fields trying to figure it out. At last I understood that it in no way diminished the wealth he had poured into my life. It was as if he had tuberculosis or had lost his legs in a car crash. He could have been scrupulously honest and not had a fraction of that zest for living. Without the money he stole, he could never have given us some of the experiences he did, and I saw that I was never going to have the goods and bads of life conveniently packaged. That was the last lesson he taught me, and one of the most important.

This is not to say the outer form of our lives does not matter. It does, but not for the obvious reasons. The exterior matters because it is the means by which daily life is carried on, and more importantly, because it is the only access road to the secret self inside, whether by inversion or as a true reflection. The actual person is not available to our scrutiny. It cannot be observed, measured, touched. It is known only in flashes of communication between our inmost self and another's. Sometimes it is a bonfire, and sometimes it is a single spark, like a star in the midwinter sky. But a flash of that kind between one who knew what a human being is in the Christian definition and one who was sick would result in spontaneous healing—wholing—of the sick person. My friends' father knew what a child is, as no other adult I ever encountered knew, and it verified me to myself. His being a thief had no bearing whatever.

Most people know what it is to feel the impact of a glance, an attitude, a strong conviction. A woman said to me of a mutual friend, "When I am with her, I feel intelligent. I generate ideas." I recall a man I saw once in a crowd, a somewhat frightened crowd. He was a stranger, but the signal that ran between us made me suddenly bold. Something he knew made me feel we would all emerge from the situation unscathed, and so we did. This kind of mind-meeting is quite usual between teacher and pupil where the entire basis of the relationship is a fostering and a letting go.

A teen-age girl of my acquaintance has an almost magical charm for young children, and she makes a lot of money as a baby-sitter. I really believe they would follow her off like the Pied Piper if she wanted them to. Yet she says she does not like children much and doubts she will ever be a mother. She has strong career plans; that's why she wants the money. I asked her how she accounted for the children's enchantment. "No special reason," she said. "Not the way you mean it. To me they are just people like anybody else."

Just people. That said it all. The affirmation of another's identity without making claims upon it is the highest possible ameliorative force. The children are not sick, but they are "wholed" by that girl, where others, without intending it or even knowing it, fragment them. I learned this, too, from my prison students. Over and over I found that what got through to them was what I knew and felt, not what I said or what I did.

The poet Robert Frost, who earned his living many years as poet-in-residence on college campuses, used to talk of "teaching by presence." He meant that he taught mainly by being there. His own strong personality, breathing poetry in and out, finding poetry in baseball and bicycles, eyeing his students and the world with a poet's view, rubbed off on them just by their being in the same room with him or on a nature walk. Frost was a dedicated nature-walker.

In a not too different manner, Jesus could be said to have healed by presence. His God's-eye view, the facts of being that he lived and, as the saying goes, slept, ate, and breathed, radiated from him in a field that could be felt. You will remember that when Judas and a band of soldiers came into Gethsemane with swords and staves to seize him, he asked them whom they wanted. When they said Jesus of Nazareth, he replied, "I am he," and the whole motley company fell backward to the ground. How humiliating to find themselves scattered like jackstraws by one unarmed man identifying himself. It almost has a ring of high comedy. They scrambled up, collected their weapons, and began all over again when Jesus patiently and—I cannot help feeling—with suppressed amusement repeated his inquiry, "Whom seek ye?"[5]

Somebody said to me once years ago—and I have hugged the statement to myself ever since—"People did not stay dead in his presence." Neither did they stay sick. Those who came within range of his luminosity and brought with them any kind of receptivity were at once healed. They could not help it and Jesus could not help it. Even his robe brushing past or his shadow falling across bedridden people restored them.

In Latin the word *virtue* is comprised of *vir,* man, and *tus,* approximately the equivalent of *-ship* or *-ness,* as in *seamanship* or *openness.* Virtue then is basically manliness, including those qualities associated with it, such as courage, excellence, honor. The Greek word translated in the New Testament as *virtue* is actually *power.* It is the same Greek word from which we get *dynamo* and *dynamic.* This is a far cry from social or even moral correctness. Jesus not infrequently made hay out of social and moral correctness, and he said in effect that rules were made to serve man, not man for the rules.

A rich young man once addressed the Lord as "Good Master," and Jesus demurred, pointing out that God alone was worthy to be called good. He, the best of men as he very well knew, was saying that personal virtue was not the source of his power. The young man had already put his question, how he might obtain eternal life, and Jesus told him to fulfill the commandments—do not murder, defraud not, honor parents and so on. The young man's response indicated that he understood the point Jesus had just made, for he said, "All these things have I kept from my youth up: what lack I yet?"[6] He acknowledged that the truth he sought lay beyond all the do's and don't's. The virtue that heals and even accomplishes eternal life is not in obeying rules.

This doesn't mean rules are not necessary, but that truth is not approached *through* rules; on the contrary, good rules arise from truth. We do not refrain from bearing false witness because God proclaimed it to a man on a mountain thirty-five hundred years ago. Nor even because it works in society. We adopt it and seek to practice it because it frees us from one kind of bondage. Our moral teachers make a sad mistake if they do not explain this. To be controlled by impulse is no more to be free than to be a slave to rules or habit. Spontaneity is not a whim, a thing of the moment, it is disciplined release, or a released discipline, like that of an athlete or a composer.

If, then, one cannot do anything to merit the result, why bother with spiritual healing at all? I did not say one cannot do anything. I said that high standards of behavior do not pay off in physical well-being. We were never promised that they would. The old adage that "virtue is its own reward" means exactly what it says. The reward of virtue is virtue, not money, success, houses, bodily vitality. The recompense of virtue is sheer delight, success in *it,* deeper awareness of it. Virtue is a tremendous freedom. One's emotions are not at the beck and call of circumstances; fear has much less hold on you; you are more alert to nuances of living, more fully the master of yourself; you act faster and more wisely. In short, the reward of virtue is skill in living. That is quite enough. Nobody who has sampled it would even flirt with bargaining it away for worldly goods.

The great evil of sin is that the persistent sinner loses track of himself, no longer knows who he is. Nobody goes through life without making mistakes, often serious mistakes, but the inner self spontaneously regains its poise by reason of its own design. The energies that form the soul make it self-correcting. The power itself cannot be lost, but we can forfeit the knowledge that we have the power. This dis-integration or loss of integrity is the very opposite of wholeness, and in that sense, sin and sickness are related, but not in the cause-and-effect way that so easily misleads us into condemning others and crying in our own behalf, "What have I done to deserve this suffering?" That keeps us forever off on a wild-goose chase after causes where no causes exist, and we miss the way of spiritual healing.

When Peter and John cured the cripple who sat begging at the gate of the temple, and the people milled about the two apostles "greatly wondering," Peter said, "Why look ye so earnestly on us, as though by our own power or holiness we had made this man to walk?"[7] The virtue that heals is in Christ, not in us, in God, not in men, and it is essential to know that. Virtue is not following an external code, and it cannot be laid on, so to speak, for the explicit purpose of being healed, like a sort of spiritual medication.

A few paragraphs back I spoke of coming within the radius of Jesus' virtue and bringing a receptivity. Healing is a reciprocal event, and what we bring to the meeting does affect the outcome. But this contribution is not weighed up or counted out—it is unseen and can be unknown even to the individual, to say nothing of other people.

I have on good authority a story about a man in prison who was completely indifferent to all efforts to reach him. He hated everybody and stubbornly refused to work, exercise, or follow any of the daily procedure. Finally he wound up in solitary confinement where, after a time, he would not even eat. He became desperately ill, and the prison doctor warned the warden that the man would die if something wasn't done. The warden went to see him and asked, among other things, if there was anything in all the world that he wanted. The prisoner just glared at him. The warden, a decent man who had exhausted his resources, said, "Very well, you can rot if that's your aim."

That night the prisoner lay awake on his narrow cot and, unbidden, undesired, went through a kind of Damascus road encounter—a vision, a presence, something; he would never talk much about it afterward. The next morning he sent for the warden and walked out of that cell to spend the next eighteen years helping his fellow prisoners to find themselves, think clearly, become men. He helped to restore their virtue in the strictly Latin meaning, their manhood.

What was there in that man that made the Lord choose him? God only knows—and I say that with reverence. The only thing an onlooker can say is that the prisoner did have the necessary receptivity: he accepted the vision as genuine and acted upon it. He didn't dismiss it as hallucination or refuse it. We obstinate human beings find it terribly hard to realize that God knows things we do not, yet it is written so in the Bible many ways. "My thoughts are not your thoughts."[8] "Shall he that contendeth with the Almighty instruct him?"[9] "Why do ye not understand my speech? even because ye cannot hear my word."[10]

It is true that on two occasions Jesus linked sin with physical disorders, but in neither case did he specify or probe into the sin, nor did he make healing contingent upon reform or even repentance. Both these cases were paralytics, but I am not sure what conclusion may be drawn from that—I just think it is worth noting. At the pool of Bethesda, where he cured the man who was bedridden for thirty-eight years, sin was not even mentioned until later when the Lord came across the man, almost by accident, in the temple. There Jesus reminded him to "sin no more, lest a worse thing come unto" him.[11]

In the case of the man whose friends carried him to Jesus on a couch, the Lord said at the beginning, "Thy sins be forgiven thee." But even before that he said, "Be of good cheer." In other words, there was no stern denunciation of the sins. When people nearby were shocked at this forgiveness, Jesus replied, in some surprise, that obliteration of sin was synonymous with healing, and at once illustrated it by telling the paralyzed man to get up, which he did.[12]

I am not suggesting that Jesus taught us to ignore sin or to dismiss virtue, but that sin was in itself a sickness, while sickness was a kind of sin, or "missing the mark" (the Greek translation of *sin*) of man's true nature. The creature of God's design is under no justifiable bondage. Human nature is not inherently hostile to God, it is a manifesto of God. We are not sinners by nature but because we have been ensnared by "that old serpent, called the Devil, and Satan, which deceiveth the whole world."[13]

Nobody supposes that good health will overcome sin; virtue alone does that. By what reasoning, then, would virtue become a remedy for sickness? Insofar as virtue is an element in wholeness, and it is, it has an impact on suffering and recovery. We say of someone who has been ill but is getting better, "She is in good spirits." Virtue matters, I'm not saying it does not. But a too rigid determination to explain sickness by sin, or conversely health by virtue, betrays us into a preoccupation with how things "ought" to be. Then we waste our energies in trying to conform to a system or set of rules, while health is just the opposite of that—open, original, free-flowing.

Healing of spirit and healing of body are both a breaking out of tight little shells of fear and resistance, self-protection and self-satisfaction. It is a losing of one's life to find it. The commandments are necessary because we have to learn somehow what the Lord our God requires of us. Human beings are not smart enough to have invented justice and law, loyalty and love out of their own unaided genius. But someday, as we mature, the transition must come from commandment to commitment. Virtue must spring from the heart, and so must healing.

But you will say—I know, for I say it too—I am still not healed: what lack I yet? This is not stubbornness nor incapacity. It is a legitimate question, indeed a healthy question, and I shall try to answer it. No, I shall try to offer ways of answering it yourself.

4 how can we do it?

IF HEALING IS A FORM OF CREATIVITY, what does it create? You. A more liberated—that is to say, a more mature—self; a better definition of who you are and what you may become; a clearer imprint of the original design. The Chinese character for *heaven* is a man standing upright with his arms open wide to the universe, crowned by that which is forever above him—the sky. A human being standing tall with delight in living is a truer statement of creation than one flat on his back in misery or hobbled by impairment. It is heaven to be whole and hell to be sick.

All creative work has the puzzling characteristic of being two kinds of operation at the same time, within and without one's own control. There is study and work required in becoming a writer, and yet if one is doing his task properly, something else almost takes over and rides that skill for *its* purposes. That sounds peculiar, but that is how it feels. Until one gains some experience with it, it sounds peculiar to the writer, too, or else he falls in love with it and figures he can coax it into doing all the work. He always errs on one side or the other.

I am one who wanted it all within my control, not because I was unaware of that mysterious "other," but because I was suspicious of it. If it was all ungovernable genius and muses, how was I to work when they took a notion not to smile upon me? Slowly one makes peace with the dual nature of his craft and learns that it consists of swinging between poles. The blue-sky theorist must accept discipline and hard work; the worker must accommodate the genius and give him his head.

It is very much like that with spiritual healing. We heal ourselves—and at the same time we don't. This is worse than peculiar, it is maddening. It was one thing that so infuriated the Pharisees; it outraged their sense of how things ought to go, and it outrages ours. But it carries with it this exciting ballast: *you are not alone.* Whatever your need for healing may be, you have a powerful ally. I did not own the sun that came up over Cape Cod, and yet it was my sun, my earth, my event. Without me, that event would not have been happening. To be healed, we must swing between the two aspects of the transaction—that which we can do and that which we cannot.

Jesus is our teacher, and Jesus healed himself first—

and last; in the wilderness of temptation and in the garden of Gethsemane. He healed others with a word, but in his own case it took a struggle, so we need not despair when we do not attain our personal release in an instant. Nowhere do we feel more intimately related to him than on those occasions of his search for self-command. For him, too, the achievement was both within and without. He disciplined himself and resisted the devious byways that would have diluted his power, and when he had completed his aspect of the work, the Spirit took charge.

It was the Spirit that led him into the desert in the first place, and the temptations, too, are depicted as coming from a tempter, a presence external to himself. This is a figure of speech. No wily eminence appeared enticing the Lord to do wrong; it was his own mind where the suggestions arose. We would say today that he realized he could conjure up bread for his hunger, or that he flirted with the idea of using his power for personal glory. At first, that is a bit startling; it sounds blasphemous. Yet the Bible itself says that "he was in all points tempted, like as we are."[1]

Then I saw that the Gospel writer was attempting the impossible, as one so often does with words: to write of both the inner and the outer facts in such a way that we might gain instruction. Temptations appear to us largely as impulses from within, and it is of the utmost importance for us to know that they originate as encroachments from without, forays by the tempter, no more our private invention than they were the Lord's. The mind is the locale of the temptation but does not constitute the temptation.

The three temptations of Jesus epitomize all the evils that beset a human being. First, and in some ways the most difficult, is the internal danger to health. In Jesus' case it was hunger (it's hard to imagine his being ill), but as lack of food and sickness both ultimately lead to death, the order of menace is the same. Second is the external threat to safety, whether from natural disasters like earthquakes or man-made ones like plane crashes and robbery at gunpoint. Third is seduction of the soul, the lure of self-gratification in place of salvation.

It is the first temptation that primarily concerns us here, though they are all bound up together. Any assault on body, spirit, or mind inevitably involves the other two. It was the most difficult because it is much easier to maintain a certain composure when the torment is not inflicted on one's own body. The body is not just an object one can view with detachment.

Unlike medicine, technique and expertise have no bearing on spiritual healing because each occasion requires a completely new relation. Let us say you have received a healing through prayer in the past and are now in need of another. You cannot go back and repeat the earlier process any more than you can relearn how to read or that two plus two is four. You can have a million new questions about reading or arithmetic, but there is no way you can repossess the old ignorance and start from scratch.

Yes, but how do you get started in the first place if there are no techniques? This is playing with language a little bit, but let me put it this way: there is method but no methodology. In every situation requiring healing, there are things you can do, but be wary of trying to compel healing by following rules. That's putting technique in God's place, and it won't wash. What accomplishes spiritual healing is *spirit*, and processes are helpful only insofar as they open you to receptivity. Make a ritual of them, and they will block the very thing you are trying to receive.

Healing isn't a thought-out conclusion, it's a feeling, which makes sense because sickness is a feeling, too. How do you make yourself feel a certain way? You cannot, of course. How would you go about making yourself fall in love? You can do some reasonable things such as going where there are people—a church, a club, a civic committee; working in a field where men outnumber women, if it's a husband you want, or the other way, if it's a wife; taking up skiing or square dancing; playing in an orchestra. And after all that, the one you come to love may turn out to be the person sitting next to you on a plane journey you would have made anyway or the teller who cashes your check at the bank. Yet none of your activities would be wasted. They served to make you more alive, somebody worth falling in love with. And more important than that, they opened your mind and heart to expectancy.

In all creative work—a love affair, a painting, a healing—what you cannot have is advance knowledge. The whole enterprise involves willingness to go out on a limb. In healing there are no formulas, but there are countless avenues and approaches. You will soon discover or make some of your own, if you are serious about trying it, but I can list as illustrations a few that I have found useful. Again, they are not meant to be adopted in the order given. Some one of them may serve you as a jumping-off place.

1. *Don't panic; don't get angry.* Nobody acts intelligently when he is scared or mad. You don't even begin to contact the laws of the universe that can help you until you calm down. This is possible to do, even in the midst of pain, if the Christian teaching of God-with-us is real. However dreadful the situation, God is bigger and stronger. When you ally yourself with God, you tie into the very force that holds the universe together. It is just that powerful, and it does not fail. Therefore, fear not; don't lose your temper.

2. *State the problem.* What exactly do you want? You will say that's simple: to get well, to recover your health. If that is so, you may be wasting time and energy trying to get something you don't really want—namely, a shifting of spiritual values. Spiritual healing involves us more and yet more with God. That doesn't mean to resign from the world and spend eighteen hours a day in church. It means awareness that "His is the power by which we act," as an eighteenth-century hymn says. You can serve God as a pilot, a company president, an actress—and indeed somebody must, or religious conviction would wipe out civilization. But it is to be done consciously, as God's service, not as a private career. Spiritual healing leads that way, and if it is not what you want, some

other healing method is indicated.

When Jesus asked Bartimaeus, "What wilt thou that I should do unto thee?"—while the man stood there blind, tattered, helpless, and Jesus obviously knew what he wanted—he was getting him to state the problem.[2] Did Bartimaeus know what he was asking, that was the question. You don't get far if you are trying to get something you don't really desire.

3. *Imagine the goal.* Imagination is not the same thing as the merely imaginary. The latter is daydreaming. Imagination is a subtle and powerful tool of the mind—its ability to image forth or, as Martin Buber puts it, body forth. Take time at least once a day to visualize yourself as healthy, rather than as someone lacking health. It is all too easy to become enchanted with one's illness, like foreign correspondents whose best efforts are called upon in war, so that they cannot really imagine life without it. In peacetime they go home to their desks and try to drum up another war, though they would be shocked to hear it. Human beings have a positive genius for becoming like what they imagine themselves to be.

Show business people sometimes say of an actor who overplays a bit part, "He made a whole career out of it." Imagining the goal—keeping it in mind—rescues us from making a career out of disease.

Doctors can sometimes be fairly criticized for being so beguiled by healing that actual health bores them. It is important that those seeking spiritual healing do not make the same mistake.

4. *Separate the disorder from you.* If you are lying on

the bed with a migraine, this is no mean trick. It is difficult to concentrate on anything except pain and your resistance to it. But that's fighting the problem, not finding a solution. If you can pry your attention away long enough to realize that that's what you are doing, a solution may begin to take shape. Instead of going over and over how many years you have been subject to migraine; how your mother suffered from it; how impossible it will be to eat dinner; when your wife will get home to look after you—try to isolate the whole thing over there in a corner just briefly, and let your prayer take precedence.

A friend of mine tried this, even dragging herself off the bed and pacing the floor in an effort to act contrary to her absorption in misery. At first she paced and prayed frantically, then a little more peacefully, and suddenly she stood still in astonishment as the sickness drained away like water out of a tub. Putting a distance between yourself and the disease serves to remind you that you are not identified by affliction. It gives prayer some breathing space in which to work.

5. *If you cannot heal the entire condition, can you heal a part?* If you cannot walk, can you take three steps from the bed and back? If you cannot do that, can you stand for five seconds holding onto a chair? It is amazing how often one prevents healing by demanding all or nothing.

I once knew a college student, an athlete, who was abruptly immobilized by an acute form of arthritis. His friends refused to let him molder away in a hospital. They laid him on a folded-up ironing board and took him sailing, on picnics, to ball games. He protested bitterly; he was useless, a burden, no fun, why didn't they let him die? They told him to shut up and concentrate on what he could contribute to the group. He sang well, he could make them laugh, he still had a brain, didn't he? He recovered enough to finish his education, marry, have children, and earn a living from a wheelchair as a radio announcer. And he told me it was all his friends' doing—they made him begin somewhere instead of craving total recovery.

One day I was invited on board an America's Cup racing sloop by a nineteen-year-old crewman. The huge boat was out of the water for repairs, suspended in leather straps from a giant crane. The deck, to which we climbed on a long ladder, was very slightly curved, and there was not so much as a half-inch railing between me and a 15-foot drop to hard ground strewn with drills, chains, saws, and other gear.

It was an eerie sensation. One's ordinary sense perceptions fluctuated, though my young host walked about like a cat. I could follow him a few steps, and then I would become disoriented. All he had to do was reach back and touch my outstretched fingers with his, and I instantly regained my coordination. I wasn't so much afraid as nonplused. If I had fallen, he could not have saved me, for he had no grip on me at all, yet in some way I cannot explain that light contact communicated his security to me, and my equilibrium was restored.

The willingness to heal a part of the trouble when you cannot presently heal all of it is like that. Some native capacity is put right, and you can go on from there.

6. *Stop resisting.* In some situations there comes a time to cease all efforts. Jesus said, "Agree with thine adversary quickly, whiles thou art in the way with him."[3] Masters of judo know about this. If someone attacks you and you yield instead of resisting, it can augment his momentum so that he sails over your head. If you are caught in an undertow in the sea, it is usually better to relax and go with it. The currents will cast you up to the surface again, while struggling drags you down.

Thinkers of many kinds—mathematicians, philosophers, writers—report the same phenomenon. They work months, even years, on some problem, finally turning away from it to go on vacation or just to dig in the garden, only to have the solution leap into their minds. This happens often to a writer. It is not so much giving up as taking one's mental hands off, so that the mind can function according to its own laws. In just such a manner, the spirit sometimes demands room to work by itself, and we aid it best by letting go of our deliberate efforts.

The cold I had on the train to Philadelphia, mentioned in Chapter 2, is an illustration of ceasing to resist. But note this: the spirit resolving the problem of itself does not happen until you have gone through a more or less lengthy period of prayer and work. You will recall that I asked myself this question on the way home: Would the healing have come sooner if I had given up sooner or not prayed at all? The answer is no. The spirit, like the mind, does not construct something out of nothing, and it is our task to give it materials.

7. *Shift your viewpoint.* Healing through prayer differs from medical practice in that God intends we shall gain new inner stature, not merely repair the mechanism. My grandmother had a country saying: "Take a step and you get a different point of view." In a sense spiritual healing could be entirely summed up as getting a new viewpoint. As noted earlier, it is a reinterpretation of the facts. I don't say no facts are present, but that disease is, in part, a misperception of facts. How are you reading them? Can you change the reading? I have seen a fresh viewpoint cure completely, and at the least, it provides a new angle of attack so that you don't keep going drearily over the same barren ground.

Why is visiting the sick a charitable thing to do, encouraged by both the clergy and doctors in every age? Because it brings a shift of view, a breath of normalcy and fresh air into the sickroom. It reminds the patient of something he is apt to forget in his present narrowed-down radius: that there is a world out there which is his proper setting and which wants him back.

Everyone has seen an insect or a bird battering itself against a pane of glass to escape, when all the time the window just next is wide open. If the creature went back three paces, the shift in view would reveal the way to freedom.

In adapting this to healing, one may ask, Can I use

some of the foregoing points to change my outlook? Have I really imagined the goal? Can I heal a part? What can I learn from this experience? Can I stop resisting at least for a little while? If you are so tangled up in the condition that new views do not occur, try stating the problem on paper. Then ask yourself how you feel about it. Are you frightened, angry, bitter, ashamed, guilty, bored, hopeless? Write that down, too. It helps to get your feelings out of vague unrest into the light. It is easier to fight an enemy you can see than one you cannot. It is easier to pray intelligently when you know what you're praying about.

8. *Try working backwards.* This is a method mathematicians sometimes use when they can see the solution to a problem but not how to arrive at it. They start with the solution and try to think of ways they might have got there. You will recall that I said Jesus did not heal people into a heavenly limbo but into living their human lives. What would you be doing differently right now if the healing you seek were already accomplished?

Just after World War II, I met a man who had practiced spiritual healing with good success but had not yet conquered a condition of extremely poor vision. He had wanted to serve his country in the war but, of course, was rejected out of hand by the military. He then applied at several defense plants, and finally one enterprising manager took him on. He showed the man a workbench covered with small parts from airplanes, all exactly alike, but some were flawed. The man's job was to sort them out. Just then the manager was called away, and in the crisis conditions of the time, he did not return for three days.

Nobody paid any attention to the new employee, so he decided to go ahead as if he could see perfectly. He picked up the pieces one by one and prayed something like this: "Father, knowing what is good is certainly your department. Do I put this one in the good pile or the bad?" He turned each piece over and over until he felt an impulse to lay it down on one side or the other.

When the manager finally came back, full of apologies, the man showed him what he had done, and the manager shot him a funny look. He took the stuff away to be tested, and this time he returned fast.

"I thought you said there was something wrong with your eyesight," he said.

"There is," the man replied.

"Well, let me tell you something," the manager said. "You didn't make one mistake with those things, and a man with normal vision would have had to use a six-power glass to do what you did."

That man was employed there for the remainder of the war. About his sight, I do not know. When I encountered him, he had a reason to hope, for the ophthalmologist had twice reduced the strength of his lenses.

9. *Smile.* That sounds hackneyed, even hypocritical perhaps, but it has its uses. Once when I had been ill for several days, I looked in the bathroom mirror and tried to smile. The resulting grimace was so ghastly it made me laugh outright, and that hurt, but it also

gave me a new perspective. A sore throat was not the end of the world, nor even the most important thing I knew about myself.

Smiling is a start on finding a reason to smile, a reason to be glad, which in turn removes attention for a moment from being sick. I am not recommending a shallow optimism—nothing is shoddier or makes me angrier. But authentic gratitude, if you can find a shred of it, is a laser beam that cuts through dullness and despair. There always is something to be glad about, even if it is only the sunlight creeping over your windowsill. That's an indication God hasn't abandoned the universe, and so he hasn't abandoned you. You are not outside the universe.

10. *Review your sources.* This point really undergirds all the others, but I have assumed that anyone moved to read a book like this already has a leaning toward the things of God. Perhaps that's too sweeping an assumption. Spiritual healing, if it is to be real, cannot be just looking on the bright side. Even genuine intuition has to be deepened by active use of the source materials, not alone at moments of need but as a manner of living. How shall we know what God is saying to us if we do not hear his Word, beginning, of course, with the Bible?

The Bible is a fascinating and far-reaching piece of work. Nothing can happen to you throughout your lifetime about which the Bible does not have something pertinent to say, some comfort or guidance or evaluation—usually all three. I am coming more and more to believe that the underlying meaning of the

Bible is the story of everyone's life, the supreme exposition of what it is to be human.

To find just what you need when you need it, you will also want a concordance, a verbal index showing the places where any reference to any subject may be found. I use Cruden's—it is compact enough to handle easily and detailed enough for ordinary purposes. Anyone who has the Psalms, the thundering avowals of Isaiah and Jeremiah, the courage and wit of Job, the loyalty of Ruth, the countless guidelines of the Old Testament and the promises of the New—anyone who has these as everyday companions is halfway to victory in any situation, that is to say, to maturity and liberty.

If you don't own a Bible, get one. You can borrow one at any library. You can buy a paperback edition for a couple of dollars. I always keep an extra paperback one on hand to underline and mark up for my particular instruction. You don't have to get top-heavy with scholarship. A single sentence or part of a sentence, seen, loved, nurtured in your mind, and turned over and over like a beautiful shell is enough. I have walked around for days with a crisis on my hands and the first sentence of the fortieth chapter of Isaiah in my head: "Comfort ye, comfort ye, my people, saith your God." *My* God, then—mine. He is not only that awesome and majestic power, but my compassionate shepherd, my counselor, friend, and Father in whose everlasting arms I am secure. The Bible was written to you and for you; read it, consider it, treasure it.

There are other writings, too, that have value. Any

bookstore has a religious shelf with titles bearing on every human condition. Paperback stores are especially good for these, and your church may publish some. Contemporary philosophers are often a rich vein of religious exploration. I have found much enlightenment in Hocking, Buber, Tillich, Jaspers, C. S. Lewis, and many others. Some of the old writers may appeal to you: St. Thomas Aquinas, St. Augustine, Luther, John Donne, Plato, Lao-Tze.

There is yet another source that is fun because it is so unexpected. When I was still a child I learned, to my shock at first, that truth belongs to no man and no sect; it is confined in no book. I have found isolated but important nuggets of truth in bad movies and bad novels, although I don't make a practice of spending time on either one. I know a woman who had devoted three years of prayer to a certain disorder without success. One day she went to the movies to fulfill a promise to an elderly relative, and something in that film gave her the answer she sought. She walked out of the theater healed. I do not know what it was—she didn't tell me, and one learns not to ask. These things are as intimate as love, and it can be bad taste to divulge them sometimes. Always it is bad taste to probe.

Study your materials, then, and if you are in a bind, review them. Go to the great thinkers and writers, and see what they have to say about your problem. You are not the sole possessor of any trouble, and what has been understood in the past is the foundation of our own learning. If you have no other place to start, a book of quotations can give you some leads. But in healing, it is some sense of God that you are after, and though God makes himself known to the most unlikely candidates—such as the man in solitary confinement—such sporadic encounters are not a reliable healing method. For that one needs, as in any other discipline, some reasonably systematic learning process, beginning with God's book, the Bible.

After you have acquired the first faint beginnings of spiritual healing, there are two more points very important to your growth.

11. *Review your own work.* When you have accomplished one small—or large—healing through communion with God, it is indispensable to go back over your work and see what you can learn from it. This is true even if you haven't much idea what happened, perhaps especially if you have not. To omit reviewing is to miss not only the full range of the present blessing, but also to obstruct your future mastery. It dissipates understanding, limits faith, and leaves the whole venture on a hit-or-miss level.

The laws of healing have always existed, implicit in the fact that we live at all. If they had not, nobody would get well by any means, spiritual or medical. The necessity is to learn enough of the laws to make their implicitness explicit—not in a formulary, but in an intuitive yet conscious way. To be secure in spiritual healing, one has to know what he is doing, though the exact method, as in any art, is individual, untrammeled, and infinitely varied.

When I said that each healing is unique and not to be duplicated, I did not mean that we cannot learn from it. We *must* learn from it, or a vast resource for our welfare will remain intermittent and unreliable.

The initial reaction to success in healing is usually an incandescent joy and a rich tiredness, the way you feel after a job well done. Nobody has to tell you that you have done something superb—you know it. It is also a little like peace after battle, a great happiness combined with a need for time to take it in.

Following that, often so closely that it engulfs and eclipses the first response, one wants to rush up on the housetops and shout to the world. Don't do it. Tell no one until you have savored the earlier reaction—with this exception: if another person, a friend or clergyman or other helper, has been praying with you, the outcome bears upon his spiritual development as much as on your own, and it is only justice to tell him at once if the task is finished. But then the two of you do well to hold your peace through a phase of quiet, almost secret, gratitude and reviewing, separately or together, as you please.

Here one can perceive the wisdom of Jesus in admonishing against hasty talk. Whatever it is that opposes God—the adversary, the tempter, however you wish to call it—always seeks to pull a holy experience apart and reduce it to a mundane level, which can easily happen if you expose it too soon. It is not *people* who do this, but a kind of counterforce for which I do not have an adequate modern term—and all the ancient ones sound quaint. You can observe it, though, even if you cannot name it. Any holy event on earth stirs up a resistance bent upon snuffing it out, as

Herod sought to snuff out the life of the infant Jesus.

So, review your healing, and keep it close until you have woven it into the fabric of your being. If, for example, at some point you were very much afraid, don't just dismiss it now that it is past. Try to recall what helped, whether the fear was actually stilled or merely lived through. Either way you survived, for here you are, and taking time to consider how you managed will prove an asset in conquering fear the next time. If a Bible passage comforted you, reread it now in the warm glow of safety, and try to see why that statement at that moment was powerful for you. This is one way to absorb the deep meanings of the Bible.

If you only "screwed your courage to the sticking place" and held on, at least you learned that fear was not king; that something else was also present, namely, endurance; that you are braver than you had thought you could be. These are not trifling matters. Review them. It's no good having spiritual power if you don't know you've got it.

12. *Keep a notebook.* But I said before that you cannot recapture a healing in words, and if you are like me, that is exactly what you will try to do in your first attempts at keeping a notebook. But the exercise is not vain, for you will soon discover what you can and what you cannot write down of value. And in healing, as in all art, the discoveries you make for yourself are the really significant ones.

Out of your too-many and too-detailed jottings, you will begin to distill the basic truths that contributed to your particular growth. You are not likely to find them handed over intact in anybody else's writing. What happens with a book like this one, for example, is that you take an idea here or there that stirs you intuitively and combine it with one of your own. These two ideas then become a third idea that is strictly your discovery, not mine. That is creative synthesis. If anything I say to you makes sense, it is because you were there ahead of me and recognized it. It was an old friend. You may never have spelled it out to yourself, but you felt it in your bones. My words will not be just the way you would have put it, but coming face-to-face with the idea outside yourself impels you to say it your way. Keeping a notebook crystallizes these felt impressions into articulate understanding that you can use and use again.

Record the truths distilled from your efforts at spiritual healing, even if you were not wholly successful. It shows your own mind to you and pulls ideas out of the speculative and general into the specific and tangible. Put down passages from the Bible that you like; points from sermons that stir you; things other people say; events that have for you a metaphorical meaning; ideas gleaned from anything you read, whether it's a newspaper advertisement or a book on philosophy. If it says something to you, it's wisdom, the voice of God, an element in your own becoming. I implore you, don't dismiss it. No god speaks to those who will not listen.

In Moses' time a burning bush may have seemed an outlandish means of communication from the Lord, and most men might have passed it by. Moses did not; he "turned aside to see," and this very attention caused him to hear astounding things.[4]

Set up a section just for the questions that arise. You will find over a period of time that questions accumulate their own answers. In moments of need, your notebook will serve as an additional source of understanding and healing, intimate and vital. Here is a sample from my notes: "Disease is, among other things, an attack on self-esteem. Never devalue yourself." I date my entries by year, and that one is ten years old. I have forgotten the circumstances in which I first noted it down, but it has come to my rescue more than once. When I am ill, I find I am invariably low in my mind about my worth, my abilities, my prospects, my kindness to others, and much else. This certainly does not speed recovery, and when I refer to my notebook and find a reminder like the one above, it helps. To substantiate that insight, I often go to the Bible and find some such confirming statement as, "Since thou wast precious in my sight, thou hast been honourable, and I have loved thee."[5] It doesn't mean I am a paragon; it means I am an ordinary human being getting on with the task of living, and in God's sight that is a valuable thing to be. Clear-headed modesty is one thing, but self-depreciation is disease-making because it is unwholesome—unhealing.

A notebook will point up certain recurring themes that in turn disclose interests or talents, strengths or weaknesses that you may not have known you had. And self-knowledge is always power. Discoveries you have made and forgotten resurface until they are no longer discoveries but realities. An old college professor of mine used to say that you have not made an idea truly your own until you have learned it once, forgotten it, and relearned it. A notebook is a log of your journey into self-knowledge. The more coherently aware you are of your spiritual growth, the less likely it is that it will be wasted on you, until one day healing becomes not something you do or can do, but something you are. As a man I know puts it, "If you've got it, you've got it!"

Mathematics works because the units are always interchangeable. Healing by prayer works, but the units—human beings—are precisely not interchangeable. That is why spiritual healing cannot be analyzed and codified. The twelve points just listed are only possible signposts on the path a human being travels up to a last inexpressible fusion into wholeness. That final leap is made by oneself alone with God; there is no way someone else can chart it for you. The way leads to a kind of no-way, but don't let that alarm you. When you reach that point, it will not seem strange or arduous.

The twofold aspect of spiritual healing—what you can and must do, and what you cannot and must not try to force—arises from its nature as a creative process. Jesus referred to this when he said, "I can of mine own self do nothing."[6] He did not say, "I can do nothing," and he did plenty—all that was required of him—but he did it in constant relation to that other part of doing that we call God, the creative Spirit.

Buckminster Fuller, the man who invented geodesic domes—those vast auditoriums apparently sitting on airy nothing without pillars to support them—did it by a fresh view of laws that have always existed, just as gravity has. Fuller saw that tension, which resists being stretched, and compression, which resists being squeezed, were inseparable properties of all materials. Instead of making buildings by piling up concrete or wood, he assembled struts and hubs in a geometry that exploits this push-and-pull simultaneously. His structures aren't held up but lifted outward by a built-in tensional web and stand in seeming defiance of gravity-based concepts.

Fuller says, "I can do nothing that nature does not permit." To me, that is a modern version of "I can of myself do nothing." Like any creative thinker, including Jesus—and the Lord would be the last to find that impious—Fuller taps the laws of the universe, not attempting to increase them or warp them or make them do anything, but simply working with what is there.

In seeking to heal ourselves, we do much the same thing. The method is evocation and response. What each of us receives is to a great extent determined by what we call forth. Three quarters of the people Jesus healed sought him out, he did not seek them; and the proportion may be much greater when we take into account the "multitudes" and "all those that had divers diseases" whose recoveries are summarized in a sentence. Healing was not something Jesus did to the patient, but something that happened between them. That may explain why unbelief shut out cures in some localities—not that he was ever ineffectual, but that they called nothing forth. It takes two: evocation and response. Jesus said, "Take my yoke upon you, and learn of me."[7] *Yoke* in that context may only symbolize servitude, but a yoke is also defined as an instrument or a bond linking two animals or people for the purpose of working together. Jesus said, "My Father worketh hitherto, and I work."[8] In the Old Testament, God's habitual form of speaking to humanity is called "answering," and how shall an answer be given where no question has been raised? Again, then, respect your own questions, for they are one side of that holy dialogue that results in healing. It takes two: evocation and response.

Toward the end of the book of Job, God says to him twice, "I will demand of thee, and answer thou me."[9] At the very last, Job turns the statement back upon God and says, "I will demand of thee, and declare thou unto me."[10] Demand? Of God? Why not? God did not make us to go creepmouse and sick through life, but to particularize his character, and for that we must be bold and healthy. Our business is to be well, whole, sane, sound, holy. We have no legitimate traffic with disease.

5

why do we fail?

THE TWOFOLD GOD-AND-MAN BASIS OF identity, which I believe Jesus taught, accounts for all the creative endeavor that human beings make in any field. In nothing do we more faithfully resemble the Creator than when we are ourselves being creative, and that includes the impulse to get well and stay that way. The desire for healing is healthy in itself, because it recognizes wholeness as a truer witness to the Maker's design than disease and disability could ever be. For that reason, too, it honors God.

At the same time, the twofold nature of creativity—inner and outer, trying and not trying too hard, working and yielding—is what makes the art of healing elusive and difficult to learn. It would be much more convenient to have it all clearly one way or the other, but it isn't, and striving to make it so is often a cause of failure. We dump the whole thing on God and pray to him to do what we ought to be doing for ourselves, or else we dismiss him as no use and try to resolve the difficulty without his aid.

Our chance to be healed comes when we are ready to take the next step in our own maturity, which is to say our liberty—to accept full responsibility for our own events and conditions and, at the same time, recognize that it is through God's power that we can do this. One can have just as much health as he has a head for, no more and no less. So then we must learn the truths of God-and-man and live them, and this is not done in a moment.

I do not mean to suggest that anyone forsake medical treatment, although I am bound to say that full-scale spiritual healing would lead that way. But such a reliance can only be decided by each person in communion with God. It would seem to me that finding the very best doctor available could be a beginning expression of God's care.

In wartime in a strange city, I had need of a physician, and as I knew no one very much except working contacts—I was there on assignment—I depended upon the recommendation of a casual acquaintance. But I prayed. Like most people, I had had a few brushes with bad doctors, and it is not something one wants to repeat.

The doctor to whose office I went turned out to be a delight—competent, intelligent, witty. Before I left I told him with some amusement that he might like to know he was an answer to prayer.

He took that in stride. "In that case, I shall have to do my best for you, won't I? Are you a Christian?"

"Yes. I try to be."

"Then we have something in common," he replied.

I had three or four appointments with him, and we spent most of the time talking. He was full of fascinating stories about God's aid in his medical practice. When I paid his fee, it was so small, I questioned it.

"It's fair," he said. "We have both gained something more than money. I think I will give you a piece of parting advice. Never go to a doctor who doesn't believe in God."

"Why not?" I asked.

"Because you believe in him, and it is far better if you both believe the same thing."

"But how can I find out?"

"Ask. You have as much right to know that, as to be sure of his medical credentials. Any doctor worth his salt will admit that he is not all-wise."

It is advice that has served me well through the years.

Sometimes the choice to depend solely on God is taken out of one's hands—when medicine fails or promises no future, or when there is no other aid available. A friend told me a story about a friend of hers who was on a ship in the Atlantic early in World War II, and it was torpedoed out from under her. It was at night, and the woman found herself in a lifeboat with two children not her own—a boy and a girl—and thirty crew members plus the captain of the ship. When the shock had worn off a bit, watches been assigned, and plans made for the night, the woman made her way to the skipper and told him the one possession she had brought with her was a Bible.

"I am acquainted with God," she said simply, "and he will help, but you must tell me exactly what we need all the time. For example, what will be our first need tomorrow morning?"

"Protection from the sun," he growled, "or we shall all be badly burned by noon—we're in the tropics—and if your God can supply *that,* I'll believe anything."

Through the night, they stayed close to where the ship had gone down, so as to maintain their bearings, and when daylight came, the sea was coated with black oil from the sunken vessel. The survivors smeared themselves with the oil and were saved from sunburn. After that, the captain willingly informed the woman of every requirement. When they needed water, it rained; when they needed cheering, she read aloud from Psalms, at the men's request. They found an extra store of rations in the boat that was unaccountable. The little girl had a broken arm, and no one knew how to set it, but she was relieved of pain, and both the children remained in good spirits.

Most of all, of course, they needed a ship, and none came, but after seventeen days something else came—land. The crew had been navigating as wisely as they could, steering for an island that should have been exactly where it was. Boats put out to meet them. They were fed, clothed, housed, nursed; cables were sent. They had relied more and more upon God, yet each person in that boat had used his best skills as intelligently as he could, for himself and for the good of all. God-and-man. The within and the without. Evocation and response. God said to Job when he quit arguing and fighting the problem, "I will also confess unto thee that thine own right hand can save thee." [1]

For most of us, most of the time, circumstances do not cast the die, though. How can one choose or know when to choose? I cannot answer. All I can say is keep praying and living as close to God as you can, which means living up to your capabilities and a shade beyond. Keep framing the question, for it is part of creative synthesis; it holds your mental doors open for the answer. At some moment of need, despite other help, the inner voice will vote to rest your case entirely with God. But it is a deeply personal matter.

It is fun, though, and very worthwhile to try your skill in some uncritical occasions. Practice, in other words. Don't be discouraged if it doesn't work right away, for the necessary conviction and energy can be hard to muster when nothing very vital is at stake. Nevertheless, practice does develop ability, as in any other pursuit. You become more comfortable with the idea of trusting God and your own knowledge of him; you get better at listening to your inner voice—and his; you acquire confidence in what you are doing. And one day, in some medium-urgent situation, you will find yourself breaking through into new comprehension and healing. It will seem like a miracle, and at the same time a homecoming—natural, almost ordinary.

Then a little too ordinary, for within minutes the inner voice sets up a racket: the healing might have happened anyway; you can't be sure prayer had anything to do with it; besides, it wasn't all that world-shattering, what were you so concerned about? The swiftness of this argument takes my breath away. It is one of the tempter's cleverest tricks, causing us to scuttle our own successes. It sounds so very plausible. We do well to be wary of superstition and credulity; God doesn't want that either. But we ought to be equally on guard against the glib conclusion that, after all, we could have done very nicely without God. This is not just casual bad manners. It is a cunning version of the third temptation in the wilderness, the seduction of the soul. Self-sufficiency seems just as effective as divine aid, and more flattering—as if one's own right hand had some other source than God. *Satan* is a Hebrew word meaning adversary, the contrary one, or opposer. The tempter is a talker, and he talks against you and against God. By this you may always know him.

We still set divine action over against everyday human living and will settle for nothing less than an angel with a flaming sword as proof that our prayer was heard. Fiery angels being infrequent, we miss the healing that is right before us or continually explain away the healings we get, until our capacities are dulled, and it takes long toil to regain them.

If you would receive answers to your prayers, don't enter a counterplea the moment the pressure is off and the sickness abates. Don't weasel away recovery just because it did not occur in some meteoric fashion. What do you want, healing or headlines? Don't negate the whole process when you are between crises. Spiritual healing *ought* to be perfectly natural, and in a sense, the less spectacular it is, the better evidence it offers of our approaching that liberty where healing is as spontaneous with us as it was with Christ Jesus.

We may fail in our efforts because we are conditioned to expect instant everything. You won't get it in creative work. I once told Robert Frost I was working on my first sonnet and finding it very hard going.

He fixed me with his quizzical look. "How long have you been at it?"

"Off and on, about three months."

"Might be all right," he said. "Some people want to write a sonnet in twenty minutes." He paused. "Or less."

It took me seven years to get it the way I thought it ought to go, and then it was published. Many people, like Frost's capsule poets, are not willing to go through a difficult stage to get to a better one, but that is the infinite way. But look here, you will say, if one is dying or in pain, it is no time to be learning a craft. I agree, and it is a powerful reason to work at it when one is not in a crunch.

Not long ago a clergyman asked my aid in preparing some of his sermons for magazine publication. He was a beguiling speaker, and his parishioners felt there could be a wider audience for his homilies. I read his manuscripts and explained that cold print lacked his persuasive personality. For the popular press he needed to flesh out his ideas with some illustrations and transitions.

"I couldn't do that," he said. "That's too much like work, and I'm busy. Let the editors add some light touches if they want them."

"They won't," I said. "They're editors, not writers." I suggested he had better confine himself to religious markets.

"No, no," he protested. "That isn't the idea at all. I want to reach people who don't go to church. Magazines should be glad to get my material. It's just what they need."

Week after week, as his offerings were rejected, he would call me for commiseration, and deliver a brief diatribe on the low caliber of magazines, the shoddiness of the material they printed, the ineptitude of most writers, and so on. One day he took me out to lunch and said, "Now, tell me about this crazy publishing world. It's very difficult, isn't it?"

I think the Lord must sometimes feel as baffled by humanity's demands as I did with that clergyman's request. I wanted to help, but I didn't even know where to start. He did not want me to teach him to write; he wanted me to open doors in solid rock, like Ali Baba.

Of course we want healing, but will we put up with the work of getting there? Do we want *spiritual* healing, which means also insight and commitment and growing pains? If one is granted only miracles of sudden recovery that are completely un-understood, you are left exactly where you were before you got sick, and the main point is lacking. God's succor is not just an isolated bounty. It is meant to grow us up, to deepen our knowledge of who we are and who God is, to increase our joy, to widen our vision. We are engaged in nothing less than the making of our own souls, and it is not a fast or perfunctory accomplishment.

Failure to achieve healing can be caused by an infatuation with dictating the terms of healing. God has other means than carving a canyon through the waters. Sometimes there is a bridge just around the next turning, and he leads us on to perceive it. Perhaps it is a pile of logs with which to build a raft, or even a forest where we are to chop down our own logs. There might be a ferry, or a lifeline stretched across. You might get wet, but you would reach the other side alive.

You will recall in II Kings the Syrian officer Naaman, who was a leper. He drove his chariot up to the door of Elisha the prophet to ask for cure. Elisha sent a message out to him to wash seven times in the river Jordan. Naaman was indignant. What sort of miracle was that? He bathed often in Damascus rivers, and it didn't cure leprosy. He went away muttering, "I thought, he will surely come out to me, and stand, and call on the name of the Lord his God, and strike his hand over the place, and recover the leper."[2] Naaman had it all planned, and it was going to be sensational. Fortunately his servants persuaded him to give the simple instructions a trial, and he was healed.

We build in failure if we constantly try to work outside our range. As I said earlier, if you begin by trying to hurl a mountain into the sea, you aren't likely to succeed. You just might, owing to a special constellation of circumstances, but that would be a felicitous occurrence and not yet a skill. The Scriptures assure us that there is nothing too hard for God, but that doesn't mean that anybody can do anything at any stage of development. So keep your expectations reasonable. You will, if you are sincere, get quite enough miracles to satisfy and expand your range, and they will not go flat somewhere in the middle.

Failure can come from the idea that prayer is something we say rather than something we do. I remember vividly the occasion when this was brought home to me. Eight weeks after the assassination of John F. Kennedy in Dallas, an editor sent me to Texas to get the story of Mrs. John B. Connally, wife of the governor at that time, who had been a passenger in the car in which the President was killed and the governor badly wounded.

I took her moment by moment through the events of that dark day, and it was not altogether an easy thing to do. It must have been worse for her. I was, after all, making her relive something she would just as soon forget. We had reached the point where she was standing in a hospital corridor outside an emergency operating room, stunned, covered with blood, waiting to know whether her husband would live or die.

I asked "Did you pray?"

She said in a faraway voice, "No . . ." I must have looked a little strange, because she focused on my face and added, "Look, we are religious people. Either your whole life is a prayer, or it is not."

That short sentence pulled a lot of things together for me. I had long known that you could not pray one way and live another with any degree of success, but I had not really stopped to think that living was in itself a very real kind of prayer. Getting up every day, doing one's job, finding and giving reasons to be happy, imposing some kind of order on the days, praising a child, exchanging ideas with a friend, hanging out the wash, sharing a meal, walking on the beach—every bit of it is prayer, known to God. It makes blissful sense if heaven and earth are a created unit, and they are. The Bible says so. The pattern of our days is the underlying prayer we all speak without words. To live gladly and truly, whether the way is smooth or rough, is to praise God; to live drearily and resentfully is to despise him.

I had also long realized that the healings of Jesus were not caused by anything that he said, and that he often required the petitioner to do something—to stand up in front of everybody, to wash, to roll up a pallet and be off. But I had never put the two facts together and arrived at the understanding that he was getting people to enact their prayer, to bring into the third dimension of living the thing they claimed to want so much. There is no record of anyone refusing—can you imagine saying to him, "I can't"?—but plainly, if they had, the healing would not have been completed; the circle would not have been closed.

If one's whole life is a prayer, for good or ill, then to "pray without ceasing" is something one does all the time, wittingly or unwittingly. If the answers to our sincerest words are negative or absent, perhaps we should look to that other prayer, the one we are living.

I once damaged a tendon in my right hand. After a day or two, I could scarcely pick up anything heavier than a stocking. I had invited lunch guests, one of them a visitor from Scotland. For a variety of reasons, I felt I must go through with the luncheon, yet it was impossible for me to cook and serve a meal.

I stood in the kitchen and thought, "What can I do? Use your head." I began to revise the menu. Instead of quiche Lorraine, which required using a rolling pin and cutting things up, I would serve a cheese souffle, which only had to be stirred—and I could do that left-handed. The electric mixer would whip the egg whites. Instead of opening tins of olives and water chestnuts for the salad, I made a green goddess dressing that only needed pouring over plain lettuce. And so it went.

If I thought about it, the pain was constant, but the guests were so interesting, I forgot it for longish periods, and the party was successful. When they left, the Scotswoman insisted on shaking hands, which nearly brought me to my knees, but by that time I was a little dazzled with my triumph, and I managed to smile.

As soon as I was alone, I intended to relax and be

miserable, but I caught myself thinking that—and paused. Where were my wits? I had not prayed for healing, nor even verbally for grace to get through the day. I had simply tried to use common sense. Was common sense my private possession, something to fall back on if prayer didn't work? Did God enable me to act intelligently for others' sake but then leave me to shift for myself?

I finished what I had to do, clearing up the kitchen and setting the house to rights, and then lay down for a nap. My whole arm throbbed, but I was strangely happy, and my last thought as I drifted off was, "You are a nut!" I woke to total, unqualified soundness. The hand was normal size, flexible, painless, "whole, like as the other,"[3] and I went about turning faucets on and off, picking up heavy books, moving chairs. I could have moved the piano, but instead I sat down and rapped out a chorus of "Ciribiribin." When I recorded that healing in my notebook, I realized it was a case of prayer by action rather than words.

When you come to a hollow standstill, look around for some way to implement your prayer instead of merely praying it. There is always something one can do, however small, and it satisfies as nothing else can. But that has to be watched a little, too, or it can turn into another cause of failure. Too much thinking substitutes theory for living, but too much or too soon action tries to bludgeon results out of prayer. One of the tempter's pet decoys is perfectly legitimate but ill-timed action.

Sit down in your favorite thinking place to pray

deeply about some difficulty, and you will at once recall that you didn't call the garage men when you said you would. It can wait. Or the phone rings. Don't answer it—whoever wants you will call back. There is a button loose on your jacket and you go in search of a needle or your wife. Come back. Yes, but—everyone knows a loose button must be attended to promptly for if it falls off you may never find a matching one. None of that is one-tenth as important as your conversation with God. If you don't put your prayer first, you can't very well ask or expect him to. Ernest Hocking once said, "God often is to a man as that man is to God."

In medicine there is a syndrome called the "secondary gain." It means the profit accruing to a sick person from ill-health. That there is profit in it, not always but very often, is widely known to physicians. During the Korean War I did some work on combat fatigue and its treatment. This is the phenomenon once called shell shock. A human being can stand just so much, and when the outer limits are reached, the organism retaliates. It is sick of war, and this sickness is manifested. The soldier may shake, stutter, vomit, go blind, become paralyzed, all manner of things. He cannot function, and he is pulled out of combat for treatment. That is the secondary gain: he is out of danger. If he recovers, he will have to return to be shot at, so it profits him to stay sick.

He is not malingering. Usually he pleads with the medics, "Fix me up, doc! I left my buddies back there. I've got to get back to my unit!" and he means it. But some other part of him has different ideas.

In civilian life, the same syndrome occurs. Many people feel they are larger than their routine lives. We are all born with a sense of capacities—to move, carry, dig, open, see, hear. Nobody has to tell us this, and it doesn't take a course in psychology or philosophy to teach us. Human beings crave a purpose, a challenge. Many do not have words for it, any more than the soldier pronounces himself fed up. It is apt to be a vague restless yearning, perhaps quite illogical on the surface, and all the more terrifying for that.

Life ought to be an adventure, and when, for a long enough time, it is not, the creative energy boils over. It may turn to drinking, fast cars, gambling, immorality. It may withdraw into bitterness or schizophrenia. It can and does get sick.

One then gets to be the center of serious attention for a while. Others express concern. Nice things happen—flowers, cards, visitors, gifts. A hospital room can hum like a theater dressing room. Sometimes one is absolved from tedious obligations: somebody else cleans the house, performs the office duties, makes the decisions, worries about the sales quota, pays the bills, catches the commuter train, shops for the children's shoes. Or one shelves a major conflict that has been dogging him for months.

It must be understood that this is not a conscious intrigue, any more than the soldier's crack-up, nor is it always evil in itself. A man who had opened some professional doors for me was hospitalized with phlebitis. He was very rich, and there was not one single thing I could do for him that his family and friends had not already done on a scale I couldn't possibly afford. But I liked him, and I wanted to do something.

It was October, and as I walked past a fruit and vegetable store, an idea occurred to me. I bought a huge pumpkin and took it, along with several kitchen knives, two tablespoons, a candle, and a clutch of old newspapers to the hospital. I sat on the foot of his bed and together we made a big jack-o'-lantern that kept him company for the rest of his stay. He was enchanted, and I had the bright pleasure of doing something unexpected for a man who had been generous to me. We both had fun, and we talked about it for years as a very special afternoon. Would I have thought of such a plan if he had not been confined to a hospital bed? Would he have enjoyed it as much? I don't know.

At any rate, not all the side effects of sickness are onerous and disagreeable. Being ill can even carry with it the moral benefit of stripping away superfluities and reinstating a sounder sense of values than one has been remembering of late. Yet that, too, would be an evil if remaining sick were the only way one could manage to keep his head on straight. We must go back and live in the real world, and we will not be healed if we refuse that necessity, under medical no less than spiritual treatment. In other words, if we hold onto the secondary gain for dear life, whatever it may be, we forfeit recovery.

Since it isn't easy to discern that gain for oneself—the tempter-mind naturally obscures it; otherwise we would not fall for it so readily—the best remedy I know is to talk with someone you trust profoundly. It could be a friend, family member, minister, doctor or other therapist, or someone else, but it must be someone wise enough not to condemn—ever. In the first place, I repeat: the secondary gain is not malingering. Secondly, that individual is himself subject to secondary gain, should he become sick. Third, Jesus said, "Judge not."[4] And last and most important, no human being can assess completely the heart of another. That is God's prerogative.

So choose your counselor with care, someone who will find and examine ideas with you, with intent to heal, not with an axe to grind. If you don't know anyone with whom you feel that safe, go again to the books, the Bible, the poets, the thinkers, and keep praying for that friend you need. He will turn up, possibly even in the hospital bed next to yours. One of the most consistent and compassionate of God's provisions for us is the people we meet. It is a never-ending source of wonder. On one level, we sometimes meet them by accident, but on a deeper level we evoke them, call them forth, not by our will but by our situations and receptivity, and they are to us "in God's stead."[5] (And one of the great joys in living is that of being someone else's evocation.)

In the exercise of spiritual process, we are trying not only to alter a physical condition but a habit of mind, sometimes a lifelong habit, and that isn't so simple. We are fonder of our habits than we know. That with which one is familiar can seem safer and more attractive than something new and strange, even when the new thing is healing. We all structure a life out of the materials available to us. *Familiar* is the same word as *family,* and nearly everyone goes on making a family situation for himself long after he has outgrown the initial one that nature provides.

While I was teaching in the prison, a forty-year-old student of mine was released; before nightfall she was back. She had walked up to a policeman on the street and started pummeling him in a deliberate effort to get locked up. She had no other place to go, and she had spent twenty of her forty years in prison. It was the nearest thing she knew to a home, a family, a place to belong.

It is possible to hold onto ill-health in just that way: it is familiar and the sick person trusts it. If a patient is determined not to recover, all the medical skill in the world cannot save him, and if he has what is popularly called the will to live, he can survive in the teeth of the most learned prognosis against it. Physicians recognize this, of course, and do all they can to encourage that vital flame, for without it, they are helpless. The will to get well where no threat to life is involved is just as basic. The spirit that truly wants and will accept changed conditions is a necessary adjunct to healing, medical or spiritual.

It means becoming a novice again and learning from the top, as theater folk say, new ways of thinking and feeling, which is to say a new self-image. That, I believe, is what Jesus meant when he enjoined us to become as little children, and not that we should become naive and simplistic. It can seem positively shameful. Here I am, a fully grown human being—I'm supposed to know a thing or two. I do a job, I get paid, some people like me. I never seriously hurt anyone. I'm polite, I vote, I pay my debts. Why should I start over? That's up to me. How much do I want to get well? How willing am I?

Outside a small private hospital in New York where I was going to visit a friend, I saw a handsome man of about seventy being wheeled to a waiting car by three or four young pretty nurses. He was fully dressed, so he was plainly ready to go home. The girls were cheering him on to stand and walk a few steps to the car. It was a slow and shaky business, and the impact of that man's emotion hit me like a wave. It could have been my overheated writer's imagination, but I don't think so. Anyone would have felt it. How was it that, at his age, he should have to be learning to walk again like a damned baby? Disgraceful! I wanted to go over and salute him—he had an almost military bearing—and tell him he was participating in his own spiritual destiny and could take pride in it, but of course I did not.

It can seem more desirable to fail and have company than to succeed and be alone, and one is terribly alone in any truth. That is why in so many ways we avoid maturity. To grow up is to be alone—there is no longer anyone telling us what to do, how to think. We are now the ones who must choose, act, decide, judge, stand or fall on our own recognizance. I am sure most people sense this, and it is a reason they seek and refuse their own adulthood with about equal fervor. In the same way and for the same reason, they pray for and reject healing.

Healing is a kind of enabling, an "I can" that nobody else can pronounce for you; it must come from within. Nobody else can be healed for us, and when it is put like that it is perfectly obvious. Even a doctor inquires, "How do you feel?" and he has to take the patient's word for it, pro or con. He may suspect that the patient is indulging in melodrama, or he may be astonished that the patient feels better, but he cannot *know* either way except on the patient's report. The patient is alone in his own mind and feeling.

People who have undergone some powerful experience, like being lost in the desert or an Arctic wasteland, surviving a plane crash, or enduring long air raids—or even a happy thing like receiving an Olympic gold medal or being elected president—always find afterward that they cannot communicate it to others, and they learn not to try. One is always alone in the great events of life.

I once wrote something to that effect in a magazine article, and a young wife and mother took issue with me. She felt very strongly that the special bond between mother and child, which made it unlike any other on earth, arose from their having shared the birth experience. I replied that, while that was possibly true, each was still alone in it. The baby was not feeling what she was going through; he was having his own separate experience. He knew nothing of her pain and labor and concern for him, nor could she feel his turmoil and doubt, if that is what they were. She wrote back, "You're right. I don't like it, but it's obviously true, and I'm in some way glad to have it pointed out."

A few years later, by a fluke, I met that young woman, and she said a lovely thing. She said that after our exchange of letters, she did a lot of thinking and praying. It dawned on her that she had been to a degree trying to usurp God's place. She felt she had *made* those children, and that wasn't right. In her heart she turned them over to God, and as a result she had become a better mother, happier, less anxious, and, she added shyly, a better wife, too. Since these were the jobs she most wanted to fulfill, she had lost nothing.

Aloneness isn't the desolation we expect it to be. For one thing, it is the truth about us, and there is health in accepting truth, as that young woman found. For another thing, it is a condition we share with everyone else alive, and in that very sharing we are precisely, if paradoxically, not alone. And third, each one is alone with God, always with him. God must have a reason for this, and his purposes are always good.

Jesus said, "I am not alone, but I and the Father that sent me."[6] Yet no man was ever more solitary. He accepted it, took it into himself and there transmuted it into fulfilling his Father's will and his own becoming. Think of the hours alone in the tomb, but God was there. Think of the resurrection dawn. The solitude of a communion with God so holy, so private, so immense that it "wholes" is an inescapable part of the healing way. I would be less than honest if I said anything else. But it is an aloneness that bursts all bonds, even as Jesus Christ burst them on Easter morning. He is our example. We are not yet asked to attain his stature, but spiritual healing is a little resurrection, a sampling fitted to our proportions and showing the way.

If, then, you come to an impasse, do the very best that you know, make the wisest choice you can see, give God credit for being greater than you are. Don't stop praying. Of this I am sure: God never fails, and he can turn even our failures into victories.

6 knowing and believing

IN ONE OF MY OWN SHORT STORIES THE two main characters are an American woman of eighty, ending her days in a retirement home, and a young Chinese artist. He is trying to entice her, against her wishes, to let him paint her portrait—since he is an Oriental, he sees beauty in old age—and slowly finds himself trying to rekindle her joy in living. In one scene he has brought a writing brush and ink block to show her some calligraphy.

Her one hobby is weaving, which he knows, and he says, "I thought you might like to see how we use the loom in writing." He begins to limn the ancient ideographs. "Look, these are warp threads and here is a loom, and this little thing is a cocoon, so the threads are silk. Just as fine silk woven on a loom makes brocade, so fine words skillfully woven become a great tale. Thus a loom with threads of silk is *jing*, the character meaning 'classic.' "

"Why, that's wonderful," the woman exclaims. "It makes sense!"

"Madam," the young man replies a bit stiffly, "Chinese is a language."

"I know that," she assures him, "but now I believe it, too."

I bring this up because it illustrates the critical difference between knowing and believing. Jesus said repeatedly that believing was a decisive element in healing. One can know many things that are not believed—that is, not felt, not made part of one's grain. I know that my mother was once a small child, a baby even, but I find it hard to believe. I know that my desk is made up of billions of atoms zooming around at enormous speed, but I cannot say I believe it. When someone dies, it can take days and weeks to believe it, though the fact is known and accepted at once.

Believing is the action of spirit, the third element of the human trilogy that is so often left out of our calculations in the effort to comprehend life—perhaps rightly so, since the spirit is profoundly incalculable. But it ought not to be overlooked as if it did not exist. It is the bond or bridge between mind and body, as the Holy Spirit is the link between Father and Son. Believing is one of the most exalted capacities we possess. It has a bad name in our scientific age because one can believe anything on the flimsiest grounds, but then it is the grounds that are questionable, and not the faculty of believing. To believe what we are persuaded is so is one thing nobody can take away from us. When a different persuasion alters our view, we formulate a new belief, but not otherwise. It is impossible to believe contrary to one's own persuasion.

Nor do people believe what they believe out of sheer perversity. They may cling to a belief long after they have outgrown it—and that is a pretty good definition of fanaticism—but originally they were persuaded of its truth. Most of us do not believe in a flat earth anymore, but there exists a whole formal society of people who do, on what seems to them the good and sufficient evidence of their own senses, plus some Scriptural and other texts.

It is futile and sometimes cruel to attack someone's beliefs, including your own. You cannot bully your brain, much less your heart, into comprehension. To change what one believes, even when it is painful and inhibiting, is a monumental accomplishment because it requires changing the underlying persuasion. Never blame yourself or others for mistaken or bad beliefs. You will only set up a field of resistance as unyielding, as incapable of yielding, as trying to bring together two positive or negative magnetic poles.

If believing is not knowing, it is also not exactly faith, though Jesus sometimes employed the two terms interchangeably, and there is a sense in which they are the same. Their difference is a subtle but important point that is difficult to state, and I am again going to be using words somewhat arbitrarily. I don't really care which terms you prefer, so long as the point is taken.

Faith is, for one thing, always positive; belief need not be. We never have faith that something will turn out badly, although we may believe it will. One can believe in disaster, but one does not have faith in it. Quite the opposite, belief in disaster seems to us grounds for not having faith. Faith is always forward-looking; believing is both past and future. One can believe the past has been dark and dreary and yet have faith that the future will not be. If one also believes it will not be, that is where faith and belief overlap. We can speak intelligibly of having faith in our beliefs, and indeed that is almost intrinsic with all of us, though we are seldom aware of it unless our beliefs are challenged.

Faith, according to Webster, is trust and fidelity, whereas belief is a state or habit of mind—involving trust or confidence, yes, but note especially the first part of that definition: a state or habit of mind. Faith is more conceptual, while belief is more organic, our characteristic habit of mind.

The stress Jesus laid upon believing is hard to overstate. He said, "All things are possible to him that believeth," and he cured an epileptic boy.[1] He said to Martha, "Said I not unto thee, that, if thou wouldest believe, thou shouldest see the glory of God?"[2] and he called her brother out of the grave where he had been buried four days. He said to the Roman centurion, "As thou hast believed, so be it done unto thee," and his servant was "healed in the selfsame hour."[3] He asked two blind men, "Believe ye that I am able to do this?" and opened their vision.[4] He told an anguished father to "believe only, and she shall be made whole," and wakened a dead girl to vitality.[5] He said, "He that believeth on me, the works that I do shall he do also. . . ."[6] "He that believeth on me hath everlasting life."[7] "All things, whatsoever ye shall ask in prayer, believing, ye shall receive."[8]

Believe, believe. It was one of the Lord's most consistent and fundamental injunctions. St. John mentions it no less than 88 times, and the four gospels together use it 120 times, while *faith* appears less than a quarter as often. Not one of the gospel writers ever uses *belief* as a noun, and in fact that word occurs in the entire Bible only once—in St. Paul's second letter to the Thessalonians.[9] It is the verb forms that dominate Jesus' teachings. In Christianity, believing is an active principle, a participation, not an entrenched or received opinion.

The origin of the word is interesting. The second half of it,*-lieve,* is a form of *lief,* an ancient version of *love, desire, dear,* and thus to be glad or willing. "I would just as lief eat here," for example. *To believe* is almost *to be-love.* We treasure our beliefs, for valid reason since they are the means by which we identify ourselves to ourselves. I am not just an abstract person; I am that person who believes certain things in certain ways. What we believe is not merely acquired or laid on; it is the stuff of which we constitute a personality or self-sense. That is why changing our beliefs is disturbing and changes us—indeed heals us.

I once did some research at a Federal Reserve bank on the fascinating subject of money. One of the things I learned, to my surprise and profit, was what credit is. Like many people without much financial expertise, I had supposed credit to be a special kind of business transaction in which you could buy now and pay later. But that is not so. Credit is belief, nothing more and nothing less. Nobody can really give you credit; you must take it upon yourself by your manner of living. If you consistently live within your means, don't cut corners, treat others fairly, do a job responsibly, pay bills promptly, don't lie or pretend about your social or financial position, then you give yourself credit; and banks, department stores, utilities companies gladly extend that credit, so that it nourishes itself. But credit is never external to you. It is credence, belief.

Would you loan money to God? An irrational question, since he has no need of money, but would you? One who thinks himself not simple-minded enough to believe in God's help in human affairs isn't giving him credit for much. God is doing his work, whether we are doing ours or not. The sun rises; the rain falls on the just and the unjust; the grass springs up; people recover from illness and quit stealing, hating, taking drugs; they work and love. But God doesn't get much credit. We say it is astronomy or medicine or psychology or good parents or education or smart politics. Some grant a token gratitude to God, in case he really does have a hand in things, but I am not sure it wouldn't be better to refuse him flatly. In Revelation the Spirit says, "Because thou art lukewarm, and neither cold nor hot, I will spue thee out of my mouth."[10] Honest disbelief may be better than trying to work both sides of the street.

When Peter stepped out upon the water to test whether Jesus walking toward him was a bodily reality, for a few seconds he succeeded. Then he lost his nerve and began to sink. The Lord immediately caught him up, and when they had reached the boat, he said, "O thou of little faith, wherefore didst thou doubt?"[11] One writer renders this, "Oh, thou half-believer . . ."

Believe, believe. This structural belief is not gullibility. Jesus was manifestly the least gullible of men. He was never taken in; and he made mockery out of all attempts to snare him, by word or by deed. Even at the end, it was voluntarily that he let come what would. To Pilate he said, "Thou couldest have no power at all against me, except it were given thee from above."[12]

Belief in the sense that I am using it now is of three general kinds: belief in oneself, belief in God, and belief in the world, or life and other people. The self-belief is the primary footing upon which we go forth to face our lives. It is absolutely essential. All bad education, bad child-rearing, bad government, bad relationship, is an undermining of the self-belief. You can see this even in animals. A dog or cat or horse that does not know what is required of it and has no confidence in its own nature, in its just being alive, is diminished in spirit and often unsound in body as well.

I shall never forget a child whom I failed in this regard. It happens that the house I live in was once owned by people who did not care much for children, and the neighborhood youngsters were forbidden to come into the yard. After I moved in, they took a special delight in visiting a place that had so long been off-limits. As a career woman, I was somewhat mysterious and interesting to them, and it grew to be a friendship on both sides. Occasionally they would bring a visitor or newcomer with them. Over a period of about three months, there was in the group a boy of eight or so whose family had drifted into the area and then drifted out. He was not a pleasant child. He wasn't incorrigible or a bully, but he did not fit in. He was of medium size, but much weaker than the others and could not shinny up poles or chin himself, and he whined constantly. When a much younger child fell and scraped her knee, and I was comforting her, the misfit lad at once pulled my arm for attention and started telling me how he had fallen from the flying rings at school that day, imploring me to regard an invisible bruise. When the other boys displayed their bicycle feats or climbed trees for my admiration, this child would whimper, "I can't do that," or beseech me to lift him into the tree, though he was much too heavy for me to lift. His coordination was poor. He could not hop.

I knew nothing of his people, but it was beyond question that the boy had no self-belief, and to my everlasting shame, I did not help him. I am not saying his welfare hinged on me or that I could have made a total change, but I could have contributed, and I did not. I was busy, he wasn't my responsibility, it might even have been a bit nosey of me to intrude—but the truth is, I didn't like the child enough to try.

Very soon the family moved away, and I at least have been conscious of not making the same mistake again. It is a terrible thing to have one's self-belief corroded. Everyone starts out with this self-sense, and it can only be lost through deprivation, either deliberate or careless. What that little boy needed was simply a sense of being somebody, not of super-powers or perfection, but of a right to exist with a capacity to develop in some direction, *to make mistakes safely*. More than any other one thing, that's what self-belief is.

A man under whose tutelage my own self-belief expanded used to compliment me occasionally upon some achievement, and I would say, "But I've got so much to learn."

"Yes!" he would reply almost rapturously. "May you go on learning it."

Living *is* learning, and vice versa. The self-believers are those who find their own learning an adventure, even when it is full of setbacks and wrong turnings. The only disgrace is refusing to learn, shutting oneself against one's own becoming, and people do that only out of fear and loss: they no longer believe in themselves as selves. The very nature of infinity, in which we are living, is to go on developing. That is why we can never know all there is; and equally that's why not to know all is in no way shameful. To go on learning is to go with, not against, the forces of infinity, or being, and that is health.

When Jesus asked those two blind men, "Believe ye that I am able to do this?"[13] he did not specify what "this" was—nor had they asked him for sight, only for mercy. What was he asking them, if not to acknowledge that a different state of affairs was possible? Unless we believe in possibility, in life, events, the world at large, we do not really believe in changed circumstances, and what we do not believe we cannot have.

People who find life meaningless and a threat generally do so because it suits them. They can give you a dozen deadly logical reasons why life is a bore, a terror, a trap—or no reason at all; they will say that is just the way life is—and all of it absolves them from making effort in their own behalf. I often want to say to the world-negators, if you find no joy or satisfaction in this present life, what in heaven's name makes you think you would find it in another? Sourness against the world in which we find ourselves betrays a self-dislike so deep that no change or growth is possible. In the most heinous conditions of modern times—the concentration camps of Nazi Europe—the believers found the will to concoct a secret flag from scraps of clothing; to transcribe on purloined paper all the Scripture and poetry they could recall; to contrive, somehow, a birthday party for a child.

Believing is half of the world we live in. One who is sick of the world is sick of himself, too. If he merely takes that self elsewhere, he will encounter the same world and the same sickness all over again. As the poet Louis Ginsberg discovered when the world dazzled him with its beauty, "Until I knew, until I knew/ I was the world I wandered through."[14] And so are we.

When Jesus said, "Believe on me" as the essence of life, he was, it seems to me, enjoining upon us something more than a heavenly faith. He was the Son of God, and all Christians readily accord him that status, but his own habitual term for himself was Son of man. To believe in him means believing in man—in his reality, worth, beauty, relation to God; believing in cheerful, fallible men and women; in short, believing in ourselves.

St. John writes, "Now when he was in Jerusalem at the passover, in the feast day, many believed on his name, when they saw the miracles which he did. But Jesus . . . needed not that any should testify of man: for he knew what was in man."[15] Jesus said, "Ye believe in God, believe also in me."[16] Believe, believe.

Unless one believes in man, in oneself, there is no way to heal him—there is nothing to "whole." If we believe only in a neurophysiological mechanism with a highly refined computer inside, there is no wholeness to be restored. Nobody heals an engine. It is cleaned, tuned, nicely balanced to tick over smoothly, and in due course it is brought in for readjustment—until it wears out and we junk it for a new model.

It is usual to speak of disease as a stuff in and of itself, almost as a consciousness prowling around in search of bodies to afflict. I think, though I am by no means certain, that most doctors today do credit disease with being an entity. But this is rather curious. We never encounter disease in the abstract, only in expressed form, in some body. Researchers do not discover a new disease waiting to happen. Some diseases that once plagued mankind have been virtually wiped out, such as smallpox. If disease is a thing in itself, what becomes of it when it is extinguished? It has no burial place, it does not remain as a dead ruin, like a bombed-out building or a fossil.

In a recent news broadcast about Rocky Mountain spotted fever, it was said that there were samples of the disease in a hospital laboratory, but that none of the employees had contracted it. Maybe it meant that there were viruses that carry the fever in the lab, in which case that should have been stated, but can one really have samples of fever or arthritis or cancer or hypertension independent of a body undergoing them?

There was once an argument among medical men that even the turbulence of the body was not yet the disease itself; it was only the organism's fight against the disease. This is mostly scoffed at now. It seemed like saying the battle was not the war, or as one writer put it, that the bullet did not kill the man, the hand that fired the gun killed him. Yet it isn't exactly as foolish as that sounds. It is possible to win battles and lose the war, and there are authentic cases on record of people who survived being shot by a firing squad. War is not battles alone, and bullets don't always kill.

The point I would make is that we surmise much of what we think is known about disease, and so do professional men. A lot of this conjecture arises from an expedience of language. It is currently common to speak of poverty as if it were a self-contained entity, too, with power to invade people's homes and affairs without their consent. That is only marginally believed at present, but if we go on talking that way for another thousand years, poverty could easily slide over into having an assumed personality, as is now accorded to disease.

We often speak of music, art, dance, science, architecture, or cooking as having the characteristics of persons. This is a kind of shorthand that everyone more or less understands, but you can already find early traces of their wandering into status as a self-existent paradigm. Every day in the press one encounters some such statement as, "Science says that in 500 years we shall all be living underground," and it has an awesome ring of authority, as if science were a super-being with opinions and voice to which we can only submit.

What we believe is the pith and marrow around which everything else about us takes form. If you believe in God's existence and care, never let anyone destroy it through rationalization and what St. Paul called "science falsely so called."[17] Know what you believe and deepen its foundations—Jesus said to build upon a rock—but never fear to match your belief against the very best that science has to offer. It, too, is structured on belief, and some of those beliefs are as porous as a sieve.

In its relation to healing, belief is that moment when prayer switches over from petition to realization, when what you have been praying for ceases to be hope and comes home to you as fact. It may be so thorough that health is total and immediate, as it was when Jesus Christ was doing the healing. More usually, in my experience anyway, it takes some little time before the physical transformation is complete, or may even be seen to have begun. Nevertheless, the healing is actualized in that flash-point of belief when you are persuaded it is so.

This point can be so fleeting that you at once doubt it ever occurred, but don't let that appearance fool you, nor be dismayed by doubt. Even Jesus cried at a moment of rushing darkness, "Why hast thou forsaken me?" [18] The enemy of belief is not doubt but suspicion, the temptation to sneer at belief as a real or active element, just because it was brief or seems buried by events. In contrast, that millisecond fusion of faith and reason, spirit and body, may leave you gasping, with a major healing on your hands, like someone tossed up on the beach by stormy waves, alive and safe and having no clear idea how he got there. Accept it, bow to it, savor it, but don't fight it. It is perfectly all right to ask questions, but ask them of God and yourself. Reflect as much as you like, but the moment you find yourself explaining the healing away, or the questions making you argumentative or angry, stop right there and reaccept the healing with gratitude.

Belief is not point-to-point reasoning; it is an access of vision. And belief can break down if you try too hard to contain it. Let it go free. It helped to attain the healed state in which you presently find yourself, and a new belief is now required of you anyway. Not right this minute, but from the new plateau upon which you have emerged. I repeat: I am not saying we ought not to learn from healings, whatever way they are attained, but that much of this learning is tacit, not computed. I don't suppose a butterfly concerns itself overmuch with how it used to be a worm and what clever moves enabled it to grow wings and colors and antennae. A problem solved does not hang around even as a solved problem; it simply vanishes. The new plateau has its own glories—and its own problems, its own new questions. Perhaps that is what the Lord meant by saying, "Sufficient unto the day is the evil thereof."[19]

He also said, "Which of you by taking thought can add one cubit to your stature?"[20] Obviously one cannot adopt a position and make himself believe it. In an experiment with mental suggestion at Columbia University some years ago, volunteer students were "infected" with the idea that objects they were handling were contaminated by a contagious disease. Though fully accepted intellectually, the suggestion produced no symptoms unless the student felt some emotion regarding it—fear or loathing or helplessness or anger or even a smug determination to outwit it by sheer brain power. Believing would appear to be thinking or knowing plus something else, an emotive tone that activates the knowledge.

When we are ill and pray about it, it produces no effect unless we believe what we are saying or thinking, and the truth is we often don't. We want to, desperately, but it doesn't seem easy. One trouble is that we are not in the habit of paying attention to our beliefs; we just live on them. It is an enormous step in mental and spiritual maturity when one begins to know what he believes. To do that it is necessary to observe them apart from oneself, and the handiest way to do that is to write them down. It will come slowly. Over many weeks, as events occur in your life, write down how you feel about them. For example, you might write, "That makes me mad." Why? "Because I don't think so-and-so is telling the truth." From that you discern the underlying belief: that it is wrong to tell lies. Further on, you may ask whether there are circumstances when lying is justifiable or the lesser of two evils. Then that, too, is part of your belief structure.

Little by little a pattern of your beliefs emerges, and you begin to know yourself on an exciting new level. You will find out at once whether what you believe and what you thought you were believing are the same thing. You may discover, as I did, how much you are living on somebody else's belief, and not on your own at all, which is a form of highway robbery. That's unsettling, yet there is a heady sense of freedom and command. For the first time, perhaps, you begin to take control of your own events and conditions, instead of drifting with them.

I learned, by writing down my beliefs, that I am in one sense a confirmed materialist. If anyone had asked me, I would have denied that flatly, for I have always had an exalted respect for the spirit amounting to worship, but I discovered I also believe in a here and now reality. Unless the spiritual is made tangible in the material, the material is rubble and the spiritual is pure moonshine. For me, neither one is the case. I do not believe that spirit and matter are mutually destructive. They are the inverse of one another and can be explained only in relation to each other. One day I may see it differently, but for the present, that is the honest statement of my position. It is a healing—because a wholing—influence to be able to be honest about one's beliefs. Without honesty, no maturity is possible—and thus no liberty, no spiritual healing. We must never, I think, pretend to believe what we do not believe.

In general, what you believe is your attitude. That marks off the difference between believing and knowing or between belief and faith. The roots of healing go deeper than an assertion of faith, however devout. When Jesus made believing a criterion of healing, he was talking about an attitude, a cast of mind. I have on occasion prayed not for healing but for help in my attitude toward a situation: not to fear it or resent it or be ashamed of it or fancy that I have been singled out for trouble, and I find it effective prayer. I should like to expand that approach and do it better.

What we believe shapes our lives, our world, even our bodies. They are the third dimension of our self-statement, and a statement is made only upon a basis of belief. It is not something sudden. What we believe today and tomorrow and next week is the kind of believing that can heal.

Jesus said, "Though ye believe not me, believe the

works: that ye may know, and believe, that the Father is in me, and I in him."[21] Here there is a slight distinction between knowing and believing, though they lead into and out of each other. Cool knowing is not enough; to it must be added the warmth of believing, based upon the works, the healings. And he said, "What things soever ye desire, when ye pray, believe that ye receive them, and ye shall have them."[22] Have a care what you believe—or not. It makes the possible possible—or fails to.

7 the last enemy

THE YOUNG DAUGHTER OF A PROMINENT physician came to talk with me. She had long intended to follow in her father's footsteps, and midway through her premedical studies had fallen in love with a divinity student. Provocative questions about man and God, life and health, death and meaning arose between them. The girl knew of my interest in healing and wanted to explore some ideas.

At one point she asked, "But what do you do about death? If the laws of the universe, God's laws, are what cause healing, then people would live forever, wouldn't they?"

Before I could reply to that, I had to ask a counterquestion. "Are you saying that in medical theory everyone dies *of* something, some disease?"

"That's what my father says."

"Then in medicine death is never natural, is that right? Nobody dies simply because the cycle is complete, the way we complete our schooling and must some day be graduated? Death is always the enemy, and disease always defeats us."

"And you don't agree?"

"I don't know," I said. "It's a complicated subject. But I don't quite see that God, or nature if you like, would include one event so totally out of sync with all the rest of our experience—and that's what death is, if it is entirely evil. If death is an enemy, then life itself is an enemy."

"But the Bible calls death the last enemy."

"St. Paul did; not Jesus, though. He spoke of eternal life, but almost always in the present tense, as if it were already here. Whatever our earth life may be, it must be woven into eternity. If not, where is eternal life while the world is happening?"

She laughed. "I like that."

"I like it, too. But I haven't figured out all its implications."

Death is something about which I can scarcely claim—and I don't mean to be flippant—to have first-person knowledge, but neither can anyone else, so I suppose I am as entitled as any other to think about it. I have come close enough to it once or twice, or thought I had, to have been frightened, but also upon reflection to have been somewhat enlightened. Whatever one learns from is not wholly evil.

In the town where I live, one of the colonial

churches offers a series of noontime organ concerts every Wednesday during Lent. Each week a different local organist is invited to present a selection of appropriate music. A few years ago, one of them was the newly appointed choirmaster at a nearby private school, and in his young enthusiasm, he asked the audience to sing some of the old hymns he played. We weren't very expert, and the music was unfamiliar, some of it dating back to the sixteenth century, but the words were fascinating. I was especially struck by one line that read, "Learn from Jesus Christ to die."

It had never before crossed my mind that dying took any special proficiency. Death is, after all, what philosophers call a "given," a thing that simply is, like time or space, and nothing to be done about it. Yet the concept of learning how to do it well or gracefully or not rebelliously—whatever the old hymn implied—moored in my mind and would not go away.

In medicine death is the ultimate failure, both on the doctor's part and the patient's; in religion it is the final unanswerable mockery to faith. We know this and bury it away and live as peaceably as we may with the fact that neither medicine nor cursory religion has a clear-cut answer. But there is at least one other way to view death. If it is all of a piece with the rest of our lives—and it must be so, for it is implicit in the fact of birth—then it loses some of its bleakness and turns into one more occasion for learning and, yes, even becoming.

My concern at present is with death in its particular relation to healing, though it is a vastly larger subject.

And as I have dealt only with our own healing, I shall likewise confine myself to our own death. The death of others is in some ways more difficult for us to handle. It may not be identically difficult at all for those going through it, and our long dread possibly consists in part of wrong conclusions inferred from our own sufferings, not theirs. In any case, the death of others is mostly tangential to this inquiry.

Jesus released four people from the bonds of death, beginning with a twelve-year-old girl and finishing with his own unparalleled resurrection. He said plainly that authentic belief in him would absolve one from death, but he could scarcely have meant that anyone would remain forever on this planet. He himself did not remain and he is the Teacher. Jesus did not evade death, he subdued it and mastered it, as he did everything else. He went through dying and beyond it, stopping with humanity long enough in the interval to reassure us, in our own flesh and blood idiom, that there is a beyond to be attained. And then he went his way.

The freedom from death that Jesus promised is of several kinds. Freedom from terror, for one thing, the secure knowledge that death is not the final fact about anyone. Freedom, too, from guilt concerning it. The wages of sin may indeed be death, but that means death of the soul, which can easily be observed in any who have given themselves over to the "works of the flesh." There is also, in the Lord's promise of life, the implication that we must use death to our own becoming, as he did, and as we are to use all other events. In the Teacher's absolution lies the hint of a growing ability to make the inevitable transition by some more graceful and controlled means. It sounds unlikely that we could ever aspire to ascension, and yet in the secret places of the heart, one wonders. He of course took on the agonies of a violent death first, but there were special necessities in that, and he did say there was a better way, not seeing death at all.

The Old Testament gives two examples of this, Enoch and Elijah. Both finished their lifespan without leaving a residue. Elisha was with his master when Elijah "went up by a whirlwind into heaven,"[1] but nobody was about to believe him, any more than such an occurrence would be believed today. The elders and prophets clamored for a posse of fifty strong men, a kind of missing persons bureau, to search for the body, though Elisha told them repeatedly it was useless. Finally he consented, and after three days they returned, admitting failure, and Elisha said, "Did I not say unto thee, Go not?"[2]

Such an accomplishment is something I barely have the temerity to whisper as possible to us, yet it seems inherent in the Lord's plain statement of no death. He did not say no transition. If in transcending, or healing, disease, we learn more of our own definition and become more fully ourselves, transcending death—one cannot really speak of healing it—would be the same sort of action. Death is the last visible doorway through which we move to our own becoming. Shall we refuse or cower before the invitation? In a beautiful Lenten sermon in 1621 John Donne said God did not create man in order to destroy him, "for what man doth beget a son that he might disinherit him?" To pull death down from its lofty perch as fiend and enemy at once begins to pull its sting.

One reason for believing that death is not wholly at variance with life is that people die pretty much the way they have lived. I remember thinking that about Sir Winston Churchill, who lay in a coma for nine days when a less indomitable man would have succumbed. That same valiant heart that faced the Nazi horror virtually alone could not reverse its lifelong custom and resign readily. It gives one pause about one's own manner of living.

The first real job I held after leaving college was on the staff of *Life* magazine, then the hottest publishing property in the country. It was a small, close-knit, highly polished staff at the time, and even minor employees were interviewed by the general manager. I was young and ignorant, and I told him brashly that I did not want a long future in his firm. I intended to be a free-lance writer and gave myself no more than three years at *Life*. He was a forgiving man, and he said patiently, "I don't care if you stay here six months if, while you are here, you make a job of it." That was superb instruction, and I have used it in a dozen areas of my life.

It even fits into this question of dying. Many people fear and resent death because they do not trust life. They will not go out to meet it. They make a virtue of cynicism and cut themselves off from other people, from laughter and work and learning. They deaden themselves long before their time, and they often say that death doesn't scare *them:* it is the cheap answer to a rotten condition. But one wonders. I have known three people who made what they considered serious attempts at suicide, yet when they were confronted with threatening diseases, they were as reluctant and afraid as the next person.

Nobody has final answers, but if, while we are here, we make a job of it, we are living into reality the goodness we claim to want, or at least claim that we can imagine. More than that, we are living beyond death right now. Jesus said so. "This is life eternal," he said—this, not some future existence—and then he spelled out why: "that they might know thee the only true God, and Jesus Christ whom thou has sent."[3] That we might experience God-and-man, himself and ourselves; that we might live abundantly.

It is a harsh thing to face death and know that we have never been alive as we might have been. When someone asked my grandfather what his friend had died of, he replied, "Living." It startled me into attention, even as small child. We are all engaged in sacrificing our lives every day, and what we yearn for is that it shall have been to some purpose. Choosing that purpose is up to us. We can postpone it or hide from it or rebel against it, but we can never escape it. And whatever the mistakes of the past, God offers us a new choice every morning. If dying teaches us nothing more than the immense lesson of living each day as if it were life eternal—and it is, for that day can never come again—death is not an unmitigated evil.

Life is sweet, but not at any price, as Judas found out too late. In the Second World War thirty thousand British troops were trapped on the island of Crete and Admiral Sir Andrew B. Cunningham undertook to rescue them. The evacuation was carried out under relentless bombardment at shocking cost to the navy in ships and men. When some officers suggested that it would be the better part of wisdom to abandon the soldiers to their fate, Admiral Cunningham replied, "It will take the navy three years to build a new ship. It will take three hundred years to build a new tradition. The evacuation will continue."

It is not enough just to survive without the values that invest life with its sweetness. Until one grows up enough to know that there are times when, for good cause, he would consciously surrender his life in preference to surrendering its values, he does not possess life, much less command it; he merely clutches it, and he is terribly afraid—and afraid of being afraid. I do not for a second suggest that it is easy not to be afraid or that a healthy attitude toward death is facilely accomplished.

Death has baffled and awed mankind from the beginning of time, but it is said that no society has been as demoralized by it as our own. I don't know if that is true, but far too many people make a lifework out of distracting themselves from noticing their own mortality. They must be always on the move. They bludgeon their senses with assorted drugs. Any kind of diversion is called an art form, and any fad becomes the measure of the good life. They box death into institutions so that they can easily reach the age of fifty without ever having actually encountered it, and they call this humane. Some pad their minds with what they hope is religion, which they don't quite believe and don't dare honestly disbelieve. They expect to buy health like any other commodity, and when a multi-billion-dollar industry cannot deliver the advertised product, there are solemn investigations, Senate hearings, presidential commissions, and economic conferences. "And all the while God walks among them, patient, listening, wise,/ Seeking only recognition in alien sightless eyes."[4]

Underlying this rat race is the persuasion that life is merely a biological process with a few psychological overtones. When we turn our backs on our heritage—the awareness that, like Jesus, we come from and return to God—we have not the power to lay down our lives and to take them up again. Man without God is weighed down by himself. A life lived on a plan of no spiritual values is "the flesh" and is already sick of a dry rot that no medicine can reach. "It is the spirit that quickeneth; the flesh profiteth nothing," Jesus said,[5] and it seems plain enough—the flesh, remember, not being the body but the glorifying of fleshly pursuits exclusive of spirit, indeed of God. Medical gadgetry is modern, but the effort to be alive, which is what *quick* means, without the spirit which *is* life, is as old as man.

Limits need not frighten us. All creative output has—and must have—framework, form, structure, or it undoes itself. It ceases to be creative and becomes merely an overspill of undirected energy. A book or play that goes on too long becomes tedious—the notion of its going on forever is exhausting. A painting on a boundless canvas would lose all meaning as a painting. A symphony without certain well-defined movements loses itself in a welter of sound. My prison students asked me why they could not write a limerick with six lines and were somewhat irked by my insistence that a limerick by definition must have five, of a given length and arrangement.

To conform oneself to a framework is one of the wisest concepts human beings can master. It is indispensable to a release of power. In California years ago, a rich woman believed that so long as she went on building her house, she would not die, and so workmen were continually tacking on rooms and porches and staircases going nowhere and more rooms, until the thing became a monstrosity. Today it is a tourist attraction, and it is not in any sense a house—it's a pathetic mess. The woman of course did die, more than sixty years ago.

Without limits, things and people and events are undefined. If there were no terminus to life, would people just go on aging? Oh no, that isn't what one wants. Well, then, would you freeze life at some age, and if so, what would be the ideal cut-off point? Eighteen? I promise you, you would get very, very bored with being eighteen. Forty, then, old enough to have some sense and young enough to enjoy going places, to retain a good figure, and so on. But how would you get back to forty if, say, you reached eighty before death approached? That would take a miracle as great or greater than not dying at all. Perhaps you could arrange to preserve yourself at forty on the first occasion of attaining it, but then you would settle for zero development, not only through the next forty years but always. Would you really want never to have a new idea or gain a new perspective after forty?

This begins to get a bit silly, but no more so than the loose assumption that ongoing life as we know it would enrich or satisfy us. The Lord never intended to consign us to a static condition. All things have to have an outer edge or life loses its true edge, its tang and purpose. Without limits we would flounder around in a cosmic fog.

It isn't exactly more time that we yearn for, then. Time of itself can give us nothing. And it isn't this body that we want perpetuated, this aging fiber. Nor is it the earth or life on earth that we want elongated indefinitely. What, then, are we making a fuss about? Two things, it seems to me: identity and meaning. We want to be somebody and we want that self-sense to have some worth. But we have got that now. Hadn't you noticed?

It is curious to reflect that the child I once was is dead. She no longer exists anywhere. I can remember her somewhat, and so can a few other people, though the child in my memory and the one in theirs are not precisely the same little girl, either. Yet here am I, and it seems perfectly commonplace. Whatever it is that maintains our day-to-day identity, it is no less wonderful than would be a transcendence of death. We take our daily continuity for granted because we have been through it thousands of times, and we began going through it long before we could conceive of it as strange or troublesome. The exquisite process of materialization and dematerialization that sustains us and our world does not suddenly reverse itself and become antithetic to us, which is to say, to itself.

Spiritual healing bears upon the puzzle of death as the strictly material recovery does not, because spiritual healing does surpass certain physiological limits or boundaries. Thus, spiritual healing is an intimation of things to come. I am not saying those who die without some knowledge of God are snuffed out. Though I cannot know for sure, I doubt that anyone has a choice about immortality. We have got it whether we like it or not. I do say that an acquaintance with the spiritual element in healing can give one a security about his own immortality that sheer physical restoration cannot.

We learn from spiritual healing that we create our own context, in a mutual complicity with that context. There is a Turkish proverb that says when a goat is born on the mountain, grass springs up in the valley. The poet Rainer Maria Rilke said, "Where you are there arises a place." Spiritual healing is not negated or defeated by death, but is a schoolroom for it. Some people fall in love with college life and, instead of graduating, they hang around taking courses indefinitely. They become what on my campus was called a collegiate bum. We can love our lives with a passion, but we need not be hangers-on, sycophants having no real purpose or function.

Misconstruing death impoverishes all our living. Death is not the tragedy; the capacity for self-delusion is the tragedy. Unless there is a God, human life has no objective worth whatever, and the foundation of medicine evaporates. There is no sanity in saving meaningless lives, or healing soulless bodies. The medical theorists cannot have it both ways: if the whole has no value, the parts can have no value, none at all. And if they have no value, why treat them or heal them? Is it just to keep a segment of the labor force employed? If the medical assessment of death is only self-serving, it promotes fear and anguish and fails to hint the possibilities in that great event.

And there is greatness in it. A well-considered acceptance of one's own mortality brings freedom on a level undreamed-of before. One begins for the first time to live outside of time, and thus in a healthy relation to time. Fear, hope, and resignation are blown like cobwebs from the mind; one knows that he will die and that it cannot kill him. A reasoned acceptance of one's own mortality is the first step in an intelligent acceptance of one's own immortality.

Jesus wore his material raiment loosely, and shed it—not easily, for it is no light matter, but more deliberately than others. When he put it on again briefly, in the resurrection, it was looser than ever. At times he almost forgot to bring it with him, as when he entered shut off rooms and belatedly collected the old coat about him. Tattered and outmoded though it was, he wore it for his friends' sakes, that they might know him as the same person he had always been. It was said of Jesus that he rose from the grave "because it was not possible that he should be holden of it."[6] Death cannot hold us either, once we have loosed ourselves from the futile scrabble to escape or to negate it and begin to use it the way we were meant to. Learn from Jesus Christ to die—and live.

John Donne said, "Our critical day is not the day of our death, but the whole course of our life. . . . I thank him that prays for me when my bell tolls, but I thank him much more . . . that instructs me how to live. *Fac hoc et vives.* This do and live; there's my security, the mouth of the Lord hath spoken it."[7]

8 promise and fulfillment

WELL, WHERE ARE WE? THERE IS THE Sphinx sitting out there, looking at us—looking at me anyway—unblinking, unmoved. What have I said to it? Certainly nothing new. But that is what a Sphinx is for, to remind us that truth is old and unmovable, but it comes to every human being fresh, as each one perceives it in his or her own way. There is no such thing as a secondhand truth.

The French mathematician and philosopher Henri Poincaré said that when he had grasped a fine point in mathematics, he had the unshakable impression of having created it himself. In a real sense he did, for whenever truth kindles in a single human mind, it is re-created upon the earth. The path to spiritual healing is not a master plan that one must locate and may miss; it is created under one's feet as one goes.

I realize that I have been largely addressing myself, setting questions for myself, returning to myself such answers as have appeared in my experience of life and mind so far. This is always the case when one writes a book of this kind. I have encountered the phenomenon before. One can speak only for oneself. I shall have gained my goal if you will speak for yourself, even if it is to disagree.

Certain philosophers say, and I agree, that it is we who create meaning in the world. Some critics say it is we who create meaning in the Bible, too. This is no argument for the unreality either of the Bible or the world. Both are there for us to create upon and in and with. We are definitively those beings desirous and capable of meanings. While the critics may not agree with me that it is God who created us so, something did, for it is not Christians alone who exercise this faculty. We reject our own function in the scheme of things if we do not act upon our meaning-making nature. Everyone does act on it, knowingly or otherwise. If we did not, we should be living in a madhouse. The humblest intellect imposes some kind of order in its world, even if it is only an orderly illusion.

I am an amateur in the literal sense—a lover—of the teachings of Christ Jesus as I construe them, and I have written some of the meanings and uses that those teachings hold for me. They are in no way intended to be handwriting on the wall. I urge you, as I have already done, to adopt nothing that finds no echo in your own heart and mind, and then only as refracted light upon your own incalculable quest. "A book," said the Abbé Ernest Dimnet, "is a state of consciousness varying with the reader."

I do not scorn the medical field; indeed, I have had occasion to be grateful to it. I question some of its premises and the power structure built upon them. The attempt to have health without holiness seems to me as irrational as trying to have justice without abstract truth, which is another common and devastating mistake in the world today. Most people in democratic countries take for granted an ideal justice to which all customs and laws are subject, but they would be hard put to define it. An equality, they might say, but equal in whose sight? Equality before the law, perhaps. But the law itself must be equitable and accounted to be just. Well, then, justice is a natural concept generated in the hearts of men. But men's hearts can be very wicked and very cunning, scarcely a reliable scale for determining justice. Oh, you are lint-picking. Thomas Jefferson had no trouble with it: he simply said all men are created equal. We go back to square one: created by whom or what?

Jefferson knew the answer. He attributed the rights of humanity to their Creator, and the only excuse he gave governments for existing at all was to secure those God-given rights. The nation, like everybody else, was answerable to God. It is interesting to note that Communist jurisprudence, insofar as I follow it, does not for a moment presume there is any absolute justice precisely because, on their terms, there is no God. Justice is defined as whatever the party in power finds serviceable and can enforce. Theoretically this applies to any party that can wangle power, and thus it seems to them equal and just. That at least is honest. The trend in the West is trying to have God's justice without God, and it doesn't work very well.

Can we have health without God? Of course, if health, like Communist justice, is a purely workbox affair. This premise is exactly what I find unstable. All one has to do is look around. The Quaker aunt of a friend of mine died in a nursing home over many long months. Everything possible was done to alleviate her bodily pain, with the result that her mind was mostly blurred. One day when my friend was visiting her, the aunt looked at her in a rare moment of lucidity and asked, "What does one do when one is beyond despair?"

There is something awry with a care system that proclaims itself to be humanitarian and yet tolerates, even fosters, such desolation of spirit. That woman was not a lone case; she was just articulate enough to put it into words. A human being is not an assemblage of facts; he is a body of meanings.

At a 1977 meeting of the National Cancer Institute, a Minnesota nurse reported on a new plan at her hospital that let dying children go home, with a visiting nurse to aid in practicalities. She told of the marked increase in happiness and the diminished suffering for both the child and the family, contrasted with the cool hospital scene where a dozen busy professionals came between the child and those who loved him. The paper was delivered and received as revolutionary:

patients actually had rights, were entitled to consideration!

But those were a very few children out of millions of sick people. For the most part, the real action is between the doctor and the disease. The patient's proper role is to keep quiet and stay out of the way. The welfare of his spirit is dismissed as an ephemeral nuisance. How very different was the Lord's approach. He healed people, not diseases. At most, the disease was a secondary phenomenon, and he kept it in its place.

Yet if Jesus intended us to obtain healing by spiritual means, why didn't he leave us an exact system? Quite simply, because there is none. An individual's correlation to God is unique, secret, sacred. When Jesus' disciples told him they had come upon a man performing cures in his name, and stopped him "because he followeth not with us," the Lord at once rebuked them: "Forbid him not: for there is no man which shall do a miracle in my name that can lightly speak evil of me." [1]

Jesus was the Way, but he allowed, encouraged, and at last required each one to blaze his own trail within that way. That alone is what heals, because that alone is what discloses to the person his own complete self. It cannot be done by passport, fiat, or prescription. The Bible does not say what it means, because we are the meaners. It means different things to different people, and different things at different times to the same person. Therein lies its timeless value.

Some people object to incorporating physical health

into Christianity—except for the odd miracle—on the grounds that it would reduce a holy doctrine to a merchandise, material profit in exchange for moral allegiance. This seems to me a legitimate misgiving, but we need to walk carefully. If Christianity is used merely to get fatter fish and tastier loaves, then we are indeed desecrating it. We cannot really use Christianity for any purpose—the whole design is that it shall use us. But if we hold the Lord's purpose entirely aloof from material concerns, we are doing in the opposite direction what I criticize the medical profession for doing from its end—splintering human nature, breaking it up instead of unifying it, and falling into the old trap of making heaven one thing and earth quite another.

Nothing so staggers a Christian as the discovery that he, too, must be converted. However genuine his belief, one day there must come a transsubstantiation from believing to living and breathing. Then we incorporate, embody, the Christ. "As thou, Father, art in me, and I in thee, that they also may be one in us." [2] Majestic occasions for effecting this metamorphosis seldom occur in ordinary lives, but healing is something simple and close to home for everyone. It fulfills all the requirements for this vital consequence, conversion.

Anyone can be healed because anyone can grow up, and it can happen at any age. I knew a woman who was seventy-five when she gained her first real stature as an adult and, at the same time, was freed from a back ailment that had hampered her a long time. I asked her if she regretted the lost years, and she looked at me in amazement. "But I *needed* my life in order to be where I am now, don't you see?" she asked.

No one is shut out; nobody is a poor prospect. One person's promise may be greater than another's, but each can fulfill whatever was inherent in him from the beginning, and that's what healing is. It is one's own particular wholeness that is at issue, not somebody else's. Health pre-exists as an ideal, like justice, or beauty, but *your* healing is peculiarly your own expression of that ideal. A dandelion will not turn into a rose, but it shall become a gold sovereign in the grass, a lion among weeds if you will, but itself, one whole complete dandelion.

If you have prayed for healing without success, don't be too discouraged. You may have made more progress than is evident. Ideas start forming long before they appear in the forefront of our minds, and so do healings. Curiously enough, what lies beyond success is exactly what lies beyond failure—namely, a new beginning. If a healing rather easily come by leads one to think he has got it all figured out, success slams the door on future growth, which is the real goal. Success is valuable not as an end, but as a stepping stone. You are engaging in a lifework when you venture into spiritual healing. We were never promised that it would be easy, only that it would make us free, and freedom is a long-range enterprise. Even after one has got it, one has to live with it.

One of the special characteristics of metaphysical as

contrasted with strictly physical healing is that it leagues one with all the world. The healing is austerely private, but its repercussions are universal, and the healed person knows it. What has occurred to him lessens by one mustard seed the tempter's propaganda that everyone is subject to disease, and why should any person escape? Since nobody lives in a vacuum, any one healing adds to the atmosphere of spiritual influence on others. The early Christian writer Origen translated *virtues* as *influences*.

That impulse I mentioned to shout one's victory from the housetops stems partly from an instinctive awareness of this impact. I heard a man tell a roomful of clergymen that when he discovered his capacity to be healed, he had to restrain himself from grabbing strangers on the street and yelling, "Look here, it's true! It's for everyone! You're free!" On the morning after a spiritual healing, nobody has to tell you to love your neighbor; it's an irresistible compulsion.

But the way is straight and narrow, which means it is singular—and holy. That was what made it a bit difficult for you to find, remember? As no one else could hand you a map, you cannot in turn steer others. Moreover, it is not going to be all smooth sailing from here on. It feels as if it were, I know. One goes into orbit for a time, but you cannot stay there. You learn not to speak your witness—unless you are invited to—but to live it and be it. In that way only can you truly aid others to make their own way. A friend pointed out to me that Jesus did his praying on the mountain tops, but even he came straight down and dwelt with the multitude. If he had not, we should be bereft of him today.

We tend to think we are entitled to health, and so we are, but our obligation is to God, not to biology. I keep feeling spiritual healing must be simpler and easier than I have so far been able to show. Probably it is, but like others I have been educated away from it, not just in my own time but for centuries. Not living in a vacuum weighs in both directions. We take our self-image in part from the image others hold, and though we have the power to refuse it, we don't always know that. The older such communal assumptions are, the more entrenched they become.

There is nothing intellectually shabby in healing by prayer, but many people honestly think there is, so one is swimming upstream from the start. When I went to New York City as a young woman, knowing no one and having total assets of thirty dollars and faith, some people said to me, "Have you any idea what the odds are against you?" I could not see what that had to do with it. One cannot attain any spiritual goal by playing the odds, that much I know. If anyone anywhere at any time has been healed spiritually, that is proof that it can happen in the world. Statistics have no bearing on spiritual healing, because the relationship with God is—and demands to be—a one-to-one experience. That is both its mystery and its glory.

A lawyer who was teaching remedial reading as a volunteer in a slum area told me that most of the children he taught suffered from a strange semi-deafness. If they were sitting at a table with him and watching his face, they could hear, but if they were across the room or looking at the book, they frequently could not. He took a dozen of them to a city hospital for tests, and there was nothing whatever wrong with their hearing. Yet the deafness persisted, and they were not shamming. Gradually he learned that those youngsters could and did shut their ears as readily as other people can close their eyes. Living from infancy as they had in a cacophony of noise—radios, TV, families, traffic, sirens, feuds, parties—they developed the trick of tuning most of it out for sheer survival. Had they not been able to do it as babies, they could not have slept as they must. It was in no way a calculated maneuver, of course. As they grew older and people began to screech at them, and as they shouted to one another to make themselves heard at play, they continued to shut off a large percent of incoming sound, until it became a second-nature function.

Resistance to spiritual healing is much like that. It is not that we consider and reject it; we don't hear it in the first place. We do not live in a climate conducive to discernment of spiritual possibilities. It takes a minor revolution for anyone to sustain effort toward a spiritusl end. In the beginning of our lives, someone else conceives us, and we are all the rest of the time trying to conceive of ourselves. What spiritual healing has to offer is not only reconstruction, but a reconception, a new image. In some ways it is far easier to make do with the old one.

The world we live in was here before we came, and it will remain long after we leave, but equally and concurrently, the world lives in us. For each of us individually, the world began when we began and will dissolve when we depart. For me personally, the world does not exist outside my ideas of it, my experience in it. If that is true of the world, it is true of all it contains. Disease then does not exist entirely apart from my ideas of it. If I can change my ideas, I can change my conditions. If I can alter my ideas seriously enough, I could dispel the disease.

Let me say plainly that it is not claimed we think our way into sickness, or think our way out of it, any more than those slum children defended themselves against noise by taking thought. The notion that that is the foundation of spiritual healing is probably the main obstacle to exploring it. We can and must obtain visible, tangible results, or the scoffers rightly jeer at us as superstitious and even dangerous, but we can never wring from prayer the empirical results of scientific method. It comes a shade closer to say that we feel our way into all our conditions, but that too is wrong if it implies any degree of willing ourselves to be sick or well.

Perhaps I can clarify it this way: Can you think of thinking as a whole-person activity? We do think our way into experience in this special qualified sense: that we think not alone with our mental equipment, but with our entire bodies and our spirits, as well. Someone said to me about an inventor, "He thinks with his fingertips." So do we at times. It is a much more inborn way of thinking than the mental selectivity we achieve later. Watch a two-year-old with a mud puddle. He is not content to look at it and classify it; he wants to wade in it, splash it and hear the sound, squeeze the mud, and if you don't keep a sharp eye on him, he will taste it. Only by such "thinking" can he really know what a mud puddle is. And the process goes the other way also: we body forth not just molecules and organs, but consciousness and spirit, ideas and moods, joy, rage, frustration, skill, beauty, ugliness, sickness, health.

The chief method of verification in science is repetition. Eliminate as many variables as possible, repeat the experiment, and if you get the same result, the proposition is proved. Human beings are infinitely various. Eliminate that and you cast aside the one thing that characterizes them as human, rather than biological data banks. Spiritual method is much more akin to the mental process that conceived and set up the scientific experiment in the first place. That was done on intuition, a hunch, daring, a good guess based upon some past knowledge and an as yet unfounded mental leap forward. And that is what healing prayer is—deep-down, self-realizing, creative intuition, based upon some consciousness of God and an as yet unfounded mental leap forward.

It has dawned on scientists fairly recently that the conditions we look for rise to meet the looking. No totally impartial observation is possible because observing implies and involves an observer, and what he sees exists largely within himself. He, like all the rest of us, is not just a set of facts, equipped to register other facts; he is a mind and spirit, too, and he thinks with all three components of himself.

We have far more to do with formulating ourselves and what goes on around us than we generally know. It took me long years to understand why Australians were not walking around upside down, and nobody could make it plain to me until, long after my school-days, a pilot explained that direction is not in space, it's in us. What is "up" is that which is above our heads, and therefore "up" is just as genuinely up to an Australian head as it is to ours. The astronauts encountered this even more vividly. The first men in orbit around the earth saw three or four sunrises in a few hours' time. In effect they lived through several man-made "days" to our one. Those on the moon beheld earthrise and earthset; to them it was the earth that came up and went down, while they and their lunar home were the unmoving center point.

Jesus may have been saying something as scientific and realistic as it was divine when he proclaimed that the kingdom of God was within us. Some scholars say that word *within* should have been translated *among,* but I am not sure that invalidates the usual interpretation. The word's literal meaning is "in the midst," and it could be true both ways. The Lord prefaced that statement with the reminder that "The kingdom of God cometh not with observation: neither shall they say, Lo here! or, lo there!"[3] If he meant only that the kingdom was among his listeners, in the presence of himself, it could surely have been observed.

Not only is the reality we seek inner rather than outer, but a human being is not a democracy and is not properly governed by committee, statistics, or averages. Each one is a kingdom ruled under the sovereignty of God. The notion that we can dismiss the core of our lives and find wholeness is erratic and in the long run unworkable.

If anything ought to be evident, it is that we desperately need new approaches to healing. And for that we need new concepts of human beings—what they are, why they are, what they may become, how to treat them justly; these are precisely the areas of religious concern. We must stop dividing man from his centrality and expect it to lead to wholeness. We are lying in bits and pieces all over the landscape, "broken cisterns that can hold no water."[4] That is primarily what ails us.

There are two views of health. One is mechanistic: it treats human beings with scientific ingenuity, very much like any other technical challenge, exponentially, empirically. The patient's job is to be meek before medical convention and acquiesce to a system that affects to know more about him than he himself can ever know. The second is holistic: it treats human beings as wholes, capable of self-knowledge and self-government. The patient's job is to assert his wholeness by utilizing his gifts to become all that may be in him to be. The first view leads to impotence; the second leads to autonomy under God. Jesus said, "Be ye therefore perfect, even as your Father which is in heaven is perfect."[5] To perfect is to mature, to develop entirely, to complete or make whole.

The gypsies say the blackest of all losses is the loss

of insight, and for that reason they never tell fortunes among themselves. Insight can only well up from within. Whatever aid one may seek in any situation, its only use is to *aid,* it can never stand in for one's identity. Ultimately, no one can make our choices but ourselves. Even if one resigns entirely and says to another, "You choose for me," it is still oneself who has made that resignation. We do not really escape autonomy. That's why achieving it is so satisfying. We at last come home to inheritance; we find the kingdom to be within and begin our rule in it.

I cannot give reasons for seeking healing through prayer. One must provide one's own reasons. If the idea seems to you outlandish and at best an ethereal hope, then plainly this is not your moment. Never mind; no blame attaches to that. Healing comes not through channels but through necessities. There is no way for you but the one that opens before you, no time but your time. We do all things when they hold meaning for us, not before, and the attempt to compel them is futile. When it is appropriate, you will know it. You may have misgivings and backward glances, but you will also have a wellspring of desire.

Answered prayer isn't a voice from the skies—though I doubt not that it could be, given a hearing ear—but a good idea, an insight, a chance meeting with a person, a seeing how this and that fit together or can be made to do so, a working through, a resolution. We must not get spooky about it and then write prayer off as unmixable with twentieth-century mentality.

Spiritual healing in our time can seem clumsy and unlikely, even a little embarrassing, because we have lost that order of knowing. In earlier times and places, it was natural. The man at the pool of Bethesda was waiting for an angel, not for a doctor or a new development in drug research, and it didn't seem crazy to him. People had been healed at the pool before—that's how the custom of waiting there came into being. That man had seen healing snatched away by others more agile than himself who beat him to the water at the designated moment. Part of what Jesus did for him was awaken the realization that no one was preferred above another in God's sight, and no time was the only time.

No one's growing up prevents another's. On the contrary, it augments it. Nobody's self-fulfillment diminishes someone else's chance. No one's liberty curtails one's neighbor's; it bears cogent testimony to it. Unlike political freedom, which of necessity stops where that of others begins, divine freedom expands the liberty of others. The more you become, the more others may become. Each occasion of spiritual healing adds by that much to others' prospects. Healing is one form of Christian love.

That sense of promise and fulfillment which the world held for us in the morning of our lives was not false, and since we live in spheres, morning is constantly renewed if we rise to greet it. There is a side of you—yes, still—that is spontaneous, original, alive, contained, untried perhaps, almost unknown yet not quite, for it is "dearly beloved and longed for."[6] I implore you, trust it, which is to say, trust your instincts as far as they will take you, and when you can go no farther, have recourse to your Maker, hear him, and inch forward in whatever wise way you can see. That is all that is ever required of anyone, and the willingness to go boldly on in company with God is a holy action. One way or another, the outcome will bless you—and others. So our Lord and Teacher acted in the garden of Gethsemane and entered into his glory.

One of my favorite Bible passages is St. Luke's recounting of the walk to Emmaus on the resurrection afternoon. Three men were walking through the spring sunlight as it gradually slanted over toward evening, the third having fallen in with the other two somewhere along the way. Jonquils and wild iris, the lilies of the field—which some say were anemones—almond blossom and apricot, silver green olive trees, and newly turned earth scented the air. That morning very early, a morning that shattered all cant about life and death and must have shaken the earth more profoundly than the tremor which, a few days before, had split the great temple curtain from ceiling to floor—that morning Jesus had not been able to bear human contact for the fire and the secret that was in him. But now the day mellowed, the crowning task was done, or nearly so, and in his kindness he began to draw near.

The other two men were discussing Jesus of Nazareth, the hope they had had in him, and all that he had done and that now had been done to him. After

Jesus joined them, the conversation grew in intensity, though they were not sure why. Like any gifted teacher, he ignited their minds. He was a most interesting talker, this stranger, and as night drew on they stopped at a wayside inn, inviting him to stay longer. At this inn there was room, and they shared an evening meal. As his custom was, he took bread and blessed it and divided portions to them—and at once they knew him. But it was still a little too soon. He vanished out of their sight.

How very like our situation. Our eyes, too, are held back from recognizing him until we are ready, until we have sought him and our hearts are full of him, until we have already found him—found him to be true, that is to say, have believed on him. He shows himself to us in the world's simplest facts—in a walk through the fields, in conversation with a friend, in the rising of the sun and the last meal of the day—and then he vanishes out of our sight.

Later that same night, he appeared in a closed room to the apostles, and now at last he invited them to handle him, for they had a special mission to carry out, but soon he vanished from their sight as well. Since then no one has touched him.

But he touches us. He comes to us again and again—and leaves us again—for without leaving there can be no returning. Moreover, without leaving, we do not grow up into ourselves. Jesus said, "It is expedient for you that I go away: for if I go not away, the Comforter will not come unto you."[7] He never forsakes us, but neither does he supplant us. He said,

"Follow me," but never, "Become me." That would not be justice nor Christianity on either side. We are instructed to be like him, but we are to become ourselves. We are not children to be led forever by the hand. We are promises to be fulfilled by whatever design the Creator has in mind for each one. We are people of God to be sane, sound, holy, healthy, wise, well, whole, grown-up, mature. To that end Christ touches us with healing. It is our birthright.

references

Chapter One

1. John 4:48
2. Luke 22:53; John 18:20
3. Psalms 139:8
4. *Crowds and Power* (New York: The Viking Press, 1962), p. 86
5. Hebrews 10:5
6. John 17:15
7. John 3:17
8. Acts 3:8
9. Genesis 1:1
10. Deuteronomy 18:13
11. Proverbs 2:21

Chapter Two

1. John 9:25
2. Proverbs 17:22
3. John 6:5, 6
4. Mark 9:24
5. Luke 17:5
6. John 4:48
7. Romans 8:24
8. Luke 12:14
9. Luke 10:26
10. Luke 12:48
11. John 4:27
12. Luke 23:46
13. Job 13:15
14. Esther 4:16
15. Matthew 13:58

Chapter Three

1. Luke 8:46
2. John 3:8
3. Isaiah 55:8
4. John 9:2
5. John 18:7

6. Matthew 19:20
7. Acts 3:12
8. Isaiah 55:8
9. Job 40:2
10. John 8:43
11. John 5:14
12. Matthew 9:2
13. Revelation 12:9

Chapter Four

1. Hebrews 4:15
2. Mark 10:51
3. Matthew 5:25
4. Exodus 3:4
5. Isaiah 43:4
6. John 5:30
7. Matthew 11:29
8. John 5:17
9. Job 38:3; 40:7
10. Job 42:4

Chapter Five

1. Job 40:14
2. II Kings 5:11
3. Matthew 12:13
4. Matthew 7:1
5. Job 33:6
6. John 8:16

Chapter Six

1. Mark 9:23
2. John 11:40
3. Matthew 8:13
4. Matthew 9:28
5. Luke 8:50
6. John 14:12
7. John 6:47
8. Matthew 21:22
9. II Thessalonians 2:13
10. Revelation 3:16
11. Matthew 14:31
12. John 19:11
13. Matthew 9:28
14. "Morning in Spring," *The Atlantic,* April 1955
15. John 2:23–25
16. John 14:1
17. I Timothy 6:20
18. Matthew 27:46
19. Matthew 6:34
20. Matthew 6:27
21. John 10:38
22. Mark 11:24

Chapter Seven

1. II Kings 2:11
2. II Kings 2:18
3. John 17:3
4. Unpublished poem, "Idols," by Michael Drury
5. John 6:63
6. Acts 2:24
7. John Donne, sermon, 1630

Chapter Eight

1. Mark 9:38, 39
2. John 17:21
3. Luke 17:20, 21
4. Jeremiah 2:13
5. Matthew 5:48
6. Philippians 4:1
7. John 16:7